# THE WAR IN MY "HAPPY" PLACE

## CONNECTING THE DOTS: LIVING A LIFE OF TRAUMA THROUGH A CHILDHOOD LENS

KARI J MOORE

POWERFUL BOOKS

Published by Powerful Books.

ISBN 978-1-83522-050-4 (eBook)

ISBN 978-1-83522-051-1 (PB)

ISBN 978-1-83522-052-8 (HC)

# CONTENTS

*Dedicated to my wonderful children Ellie and Zac. For without you I wouldn't be here now. I love you from the bottom of my heart. My everything.*

*To my beautiful friend Norma. For her endless support, her genuine love and friendship. For being there for me in my darkest moments. For checking up, reaching out and never giving up on me.*

*To Perry Power and the Powerful Books community for believing in my story, encouraging me and continuing to inspire me every single day.*

*Lastly to everyone who has taken the time to read my story. Thank you.*

*If you are a person who has been abused, I hope you will understand by reading my journey that the abuse was* ***never*** *your fault.*

*And if you are lucky enough to not have experienced trauma in this way, I hope you have a better understanding for those who have.*

# INTRODUCTION

Have you ever felt lonely? I mean REALLY lonely… people are around, but you feel totally alone...

This is me. I have spent ALL of my life feeling like this. Not belonging. Feeling different. Disconnected. Like I am lost. A life walking on eggshells, waiting for the next alert of danger.

This book is about my life-long struggles navigating my way through a life of abuse from childhood into adulthood. Connecting the dots to understanding how unresolved trauma may appear within a lifetime.

Before I begin my story, I will note that a lot of my childhood years are very hazy.

My younger self could not deal with what was happening to her and she could not process or understand it. The trauma would be locked away for so long and she believed it would never be opened.

The way I decipher this is that most of my childhood was too painful. My brain decided, as a way of coping with the unimaginable, I had to put all the damaging memories into a box. It was my way of surviving.

This box would have a key, but the key would be guarded deep within my soul where nobody could find its contents.

Until now...

# CHAPTER 1
# MY EARLY YEARS

I don't remember much before the abuse to be honest, so my story will begin from my earliest memory.

My family and I grew up in a 3-bed terrace in East Ham, London. My mum, my dad and my brother who was 4 and a half years older than I was. We weren't particularly well off, but we weren't broke either. My mum was a stay-at-home mum mostly, my dad was out to work every day from morning until the evening from around 8 am - 6pm. He was the 'breadwinner,' he was often out on the weekdays, and it was he who was the authoritarian. When my father came home, my brother and I would be on our best behaviour. My mum was the more lenient of the two.

I don't really remember a time in my childhood where I felt part of something. My relationship with my parents was ok, let's face it, at a young age you don't question your relationship with your parents do you? The role of my mum was staying home looking after the house, feeding us, and clothing us. The only thing I really remember us doing is occasionally going up to East Ham High Street to mooch around the shops. My mum didn't drive or anything so we were limited on where we would go. This is not to say I didn't do more with her, but I am just saying that my early memories are very vague, almost as though they were not a part of me.

My relationship with my family, even at a young age, gave me the feelings of being misaligned. It felt discombobulated somehow, even then. I had a nan and grandad who lived a few roads away, my dad's brother and my aunt also lived locally. My aunt and cousins on my mum's side were around, but for some reason, I don't really remember them being around until later in my childhood, at this stage, both they and my grandparents had moved to Northampton. Other than that, most of my family was on my dad's side as he came from a big Irish family.

Looking back, I realise I grew up in an emotionally unavailable family environment, which led to me being sexually abused by a family member at the age of around 6.

This continued until I was around the age of 11. I was a very withdrawn child; I was shy and became a people pleaser very early on. I did what I was told because otherwise there would be consequences. From then on, everything that was going to happen to me in my future was MY fault. I believed I had asked for all that others had put on me. It was a very lonely childhood and I felt I had been overlooked. This played out in that I wanted to fade into the background so no one could hurt me further.

My dad was the youngest of 8, an equal mixture of boys and girls, so I had many cousins, but we only saw them when my parents would take us all to Galway, Ireland (my father's place of Birth) for a few weeks in the summer. My dad would drive and we would head to Holyhead in Wales and then cross over the ferry to Dublin and drive the rest of the way. I remember they used to have a friend, I can't remember her name, but she lived in Liverpool and so we used to stop over and have a break from the trip to grab a drink and a toilet break, and then stay for a few hours before we would travel again.

We would stop off along the way to a Little Chef, for something to eat, but I remember that most of the way I would be asleep in the car.

I always fell asleep in the car, even on short journeys. I guess it was the motion of the car moving, like being rocked when you were a baby, to soothe you after a feed. I remember it would take us about 24 hours to get there and in today's day and age, we would fly rather than drive, but my dad always seemed to like the drive rather than any other way. Although one reason could be that the airport which is there now, may not have been there back then.

I remember my mum and dad used to smoke in those days and it was allowed in the car and I remember the smoke wafting back to where I was. I hated smoke and I hated my parents smoking, but they smoked, nevertheless. That is what many did, way much more than people do now and there were not the restrictions there are nowadays. You could smoke anywhere in public and not be penalised for it back then. I always remember when we got to Ireland, I loved it there and it was where I felt most at home surprisingly. We would get off the ferry and have another hour and a half drive until we got to Galway. The air felt different, like I had come home somehow.

We would always arrive at my aunt and uncle's on Whitestrand Road. This was the hub of the family. Everyone would always pop into my aunt's house. They would just turn up and it felt so close-knit, looking back I think that is why it felt more homely. I liked all the family around and so many people in and out, which is odd, because when I was at East Ham and there were lots of people around, I was anxious and it felt like I was wary of people coming in.

I loved seeing my Granny over at Salt Hill, Galway. Whenever I saw my cousins, it was so easy and always as though I had never been away. Like I slotted back into the family as if I had always been there. I had lots of fun with my cousins. This is where my happy place was and I realise now that my real home, back in London, wasn't.

The house my Grandad and Grandma lived in I always remember fondly. I loved that house. It felt really grand. It was a four-bedroom house with lovely black cast iron fireplaces and high ceilings. It was right by the park and the beach was literally a stone's throw away from the end of the road. I remember going off on my own little adventures.

There were arcades and rides just past the park on the next road and I loved going to play on the slot machines and dodgem cars. I was often allowed to just go down there whenever I felt like it, not like nowadays where we are confined to the house unless there is a parent present. We had the freedom to go off and investigate the area and play, as I wish children could do now. I always think it is such a shame how this earth brings so much fear, whether it be through the generations or on the news.

There were no mobile phones back then. I think I would have had an absolute meltdown when my children were younger with no phones to be able to contact them on. But this was what it was like and in some ways, it was for the better. You knew that you needed to be home when the streetlights turned on. That was the way it was. The times I was out exploring were the happiest.

My Grandad on the Irish side of the family had passed away when I was four years old. I don't really remember him as such, but I do remember when he died. It was in 1979 when he passed away. We were staying in their house at the time. There were lots of people. Family and other people who were visiting.

I remember people lining up along the stairs coming to pay their respects to my grandfather. Somehow, me and my cousin, who was 6 months younger than me, had sneaked in to see what was going on. I remember seeing my Grandad lying in bed with candles around him. It just looked like he was sleeping. I don't remember feeling scared or worried about this. I guess I hadn't really understood what was happening at the time. I don't think it affected me negatively in any way.

I don't remember the bit before or after and I don't remember a funeral or anything, maybe I didn't go. It amazed me that lots of people were all coming to see my grandad as he lay dead in his bed. They were Catholic and therefore very religious. There were lots of pictures of Christ and Mother Mary. I was fascinated by them. For some reason, they made me feel at peace. Sadly, this is the one and only memory I have of my grandad.

I am not religious particularly even though my dad was. My dad would go to Church every week and for many years, he would expect me to attend, along with my brother. My Grandma, Hannah, was a person I always felt close to. This house, in Salthill, was where we stayed each year and it was literally like my home for those 3 weeks.

I remember she would cook us porridge most mornings and I can picture her now standing over the stove, with a big pot, stirring the porridge as we sat there eagerly waiting for it to be ready. As I previously stated, I loved Ireland and always have fond memories of my time there and miss those days very much. The safety I felt I had there is something that I look back now on and remember feeling at peace.

I never really felt that I had so much of a connection to where I actually grew up. I did have a lot of friends in the area, we all went to the same school and I remember even at a young age, playing outside when the weather was good. With no real curfew. We were always outside. There would always be other children out to meet up and play with.

Back home, my parents used to throw the odd party at the house. At that time they seemed to have friends that they socialised with. Some were old school friends, who also had kids close in age and it felt like it was quite regular, but that may not have been the case.

One of my earliest memories of being with my mum and brother was in the school holidays. We all went to the high street and I remember going into a shoe shop with them. I must have only been about 5 and it was a clear indication of my love for footwear as my mum used to push around a shopping trolley and I had somehow managed to pop these long, heeled boots in the trolley without her noticing in the hope I could dress up when I got back home to play make-believe.

We walked halfway across the high street, when my mum happened to look for something in the trolley and spotted the boots I was trying to conceal. To my dismay, she made me walk back to the shop and put them back with my tail between my legs.

My love for boots has never changed, but I go about the more lawful way of purchasing than I did back then :)

I remember doing the usual things little girls do. I would play with my dolls and my mum's make-up if she would allow me to. To start with, I was always girlie in that respect, but that changed eventually as life progressed.

For a while I remember being happy, but I don't remember much of those times specifically.

I have a lot of blanks missing.

I remember short bursts of time. Almost like a short slide show.

Images pop up in my mind to remind me of certain events or situations. But it is almost like I remember the bit in the middle, but really struggle to find the beginning and the end. It is those parts I find difficult to piece together. I know now, that this is a common sign of trauma.

My family life wasn't easy. I had a brother, and our relationship wasn't the best. He always acted quite negatively towards me. He would constantly try to annoy and upset me, like he took pleasure in making my life difficult. If my friends came around to play, he would always try and get me into trouble so he could mess up my time.

He appeared quite jealous of me and I have my thoughts around it now, but I never understood why during my childhood.

He would do naughty things around the house. He would get into mischief often and would always try to get me to take the blame for it. He would tell me that as I was the youngest, our parents would not be so hard on me. He said I wouldn't get into trouble if I said I did it.

Looking back, he often used emotional blackmail and manipulation to orchestrate something in his favour, but I was too young to understand it at the time.

He would often tell me I was adopted and that no one wanted me. It was my brother who had told me we had another brother who had died, he was stillborn. My parents had never told me about this so the fact my brother had been the one to say it, told me that it must have affected him quite considerably. In what way, only he knows.

The baby that passed was a boy and my living brother would relish telling me that if he had been alive, I would not have been born. I was only there, he would say, because the other baby wasn't.

I asked my mother in my teens if this was the case and she said yes. I wouldn't have been born if he had survived!

Somehow, I don't remember feeling upset by that remark at the time, albeit a little taken aback. I managed to put it behind me and forget about that for a while, but this memory over recent years has popped back into my consciousness as I try to piece everything together. It must have affected me more than I had realised. In fact, there have been a lot of things that happened in my childhood that I had not associated with my adulthood to explain why certain things happened, until I started to do my healing work, literally a few years ago.

# CHAPTER 2
# NO-ONE'S LISTENING

From a very young age it was instilled in me that I needed to consistently strive to be loved. I had to work hard at it to be part of the family. To belong. When someone is constantly being told at a young age that they need to step up to be part of the family, is it a wonder this pattern carries out into the rest of the years ahead. I was being conditioned to behave in a certain way, unbeknown to me at the time. Now this all makes sense, but growing up, none of this made sense.

I feel like I spent most of my life confused and disorientated. I was left feeling like a lesser person. I felt like I had to do what people wanted to be loved and a part of something. Even though all my memories with my brother were not favourable, I still felt I had loyalty to him. He was my big brother after all and despite all of this, I still looked out for him and wanted him to be happy, even though he would do his utmost to make my life a misery.

Family life just continued. Me taking all the abuse. I screamed at the abuser to get away from me and to leave me alone, but my screams always fell on deaf ears. The abuse had escalated to sexual. He would touch me inappropriately to start off with. Put his hands by my vagina and have a feel.

The more I yelled, the more I was seen as just a child who wanted attention. When the truth was, this was the last thing I wanted. Most days I wanted to live in solitude, not to draw attention to myself.

In those days, parents didn't think twice about giving their children a smack. This was 'normal.' An expected and accepted way to install discipline when children stepped out of line or were being naughty.

Imagine. You are shouting out for the abuser to stop what he was doing, to scare him into pulling away, but instead I got scolded by the people who were there to protect me. As if I was crying wolf. I did not tell them exactly what was going on in my screams because I was warned that if I told them, I would get into trouble and no one would believe me. You get told this enough times, you begin to believe it, so I never revealed exactly what he was doing to me.

When I look back, there were so many occasions where he was abusing me, right under noses, but they appeared oblivious. Even back then, I was being taught that no matter how hard I tried, or how much noise I made, I would not be heard. I would not be saved.

In the end I stopped trying. No one was listening. I was alone and vulnerable. I didn't understand why no one noticed.

Although I hadn't realised at the time what was happening, I used to have vivid dreams. Many were repetitive. The same scene, over and over.

Two in particular stick in my mind. One was where I had been sleeping in the box room. This had been my first childhood bedroom. The dream was set in olden times, I couldn't tell you what era, but there was a lot of fighting and I think it had been triggered by a book my brother was reading. I didn't read it, but the pictures were familiar in this dream and it scared the hell out of me. In the end my parents swapped rooms between me and my brother because I had them every night in that room, so I moved to the bigger one. As I type, maybe this room is where the abuse initially started? Who knows, but that would make a lot of sense.

The second, I could view myself within 5 different floors, as if the building was cut into half like a cake. Or a doll's house frontage had been taken away. I would watch myself being chased through the corridors like I was watching a horror movie. Frightened for my life.

I was running as fast as I possibly could. Never quite seeing what or who was chasing me, but the fear and the panic used to wake me up. My heart would be pounding hard and fast and I would scream and run into my parent's room. One of them, I never remember who, would tell me to go back to bed, which I did without question. All had the commonality of being hurt by someone and the dreams all felt so, so real.

By this time, the abuser had been sticking his penis in me. I don't see the movement in my mind, but I see the image. I remember him doing this several times over the years, which led to another dream.

This one wasn't as scary as the others and I don't remember the age this one came up, but I am pretty sure it was before I was 11 years old. When I look back, I can see how this had been a trigger from the abuse I was suffering.

In this one I wasn't hurt or scared. But chills me to the core now, as I consider the connection.

I would dream that someone had left a baby on the doorstep. That baby was mine.

Now, I at that point had no clue how babies were made and to me they were flown down by a stork, I am not joking. That shows how young and innocent I was, but clearly my subconscious must have pieced it all together in its own way, unbeknown to me.

When I really think about the things that happened to me, I shudder to think how I managed to cope with all the heaviness. Carrying this all around. How on earth am I still here to tell the tale?

It is only now, in my late forties, that I understand the severity of the trauma I endured.

It didn't stop there either.

# CHAPTER 3
# IDENTITY

It is hard to know if I had a 'happy' upbringing in places, as any good times were jaded by the bad. My self-esteem and feelings of being unloved were off the scale... Wow, this hit me hard.

In reality, each decade that came by brought a new perpetrator into my life. Each chipping away at my identity, the essence of who I really am.

I will talk about this in more detail later in the book.

I remember even in my drawings growing up, I would paint or draw a picture and I remember many of those pictures being fantasy based. I would change my name and fantasise about being anyone other than me.

Even at school, considering I was extremely shy, I could act in plays. I have put that down to wanting to bury what was happening to me.

It was safe to pretend I was someone else. I did this a lot. At school I had friends but I was never the 'cool girl', and in those days girls would fall out left right and centre. All the other girls would take sides. The whole class would be divided. Being the people pleaser I was, I became a follower, never the lead. I didn't feel good enough to be in the centre of it all. This carried out in most of my life. Patterns repeating. Over and over again.

I was terribly shy as a child. I remember whenever my parents had a party or friends over, even when it was family, I would make sure I was upstairs in my room before they arrived. I would dread having to be around them. I would stay upstairs until the last possible minute before my mum inevitably called for me to come down and spend the evening with them. One of the adults would talk to me and I would feel embarrassed and want to hide away. I could never understand why this was, but I remember the feelings I had and to be honest, these feelings would come back to me even in very recent years, when something made me feel uncomfortable. Actually, that's a lie. Sometimes it could come out of nowhere, it would just happen. Someone would talk to me and I could feel my heart pound and the blood rush to my head, for no 'apparent' reason. I didn't *think* it to happen, my body just went into overdrive.

The best way I can describe it was like a panic attack. Now, I realise the cortisol was running through my body like a tornado. My body perceived danger regularly and it would just happen. I had no control over it. It would happen all on its own and this would make me feel stupid. It made me feel embarrassed. I would feel like a deer in headlights. All for seemingly nothing at all. This had stayed with me most of my life, never truly understanding any of it. I would be annoyed with myself, especially as a young child. This made me retreat away from people. I became very quiet, subdued and introverted.

This now brings me to another memory. I was 8. I remember this because it was my birthday. I got up in the morning and was so excited to open my presents, but I remember feeling really unwell. I felt queasy. I felt vacant. My mind was just blank and I felt sad. It was my birthday, I should have been happy, but I felt totally lost, I felt numb. Yes, I smiled for the camera, as my mum was obsessed with taking pictures on every occasion, still is.

There was a particular photograph where I was clutching my Orvil doll that I got as a gift. But I was not happy. I looked dead behind my eyes. I think the struggles I was facing behind closed doors were starting to take its toll on a major level.

Things were happening to me that would shape my life forever. One's that would affect my life and the way I see EVERYTHING.

When we were children, I remember I would go to Sunday school which was down the bottom of the next Road. Every Sunday morning.

My dad is catholic and the church was very important to him. He wanted us to grow up within the church, although my parents decided we were to attend a normal state school, but we still were expected to attend church etc.

I don't know what it was about Sunday school or the church, but there was something about it that didn't really feel right. A part of me liked the quietness of the church, I instantly felt calm but there was a part of me, again, where I didn't really feel I belonged. The only thing I remembered that I liked was going up to the altar and lighting a candle and placing it with the rest of them that were lit. My dad would play the guitar whilst the hymns were being sung during services.

As I look back, I recall I eventually didn't want to go Sunday school and I remember crying before I was due to go. This happened often. Later, when I stopped going, my father wanted to take me and my brother to church with him on a Sunday instead and we both used to pretend to be fast asleep when my father came in. Eventually over the months, he gave up and stopped bothering getting us up to go.

My father, I think, was the more active parent on the weekends with us. I seem to remember if we were to go to the park, or swimming or even ice skating, it was my dad who would take us. We used to go swimming every Friday to Greenwich Baths (the 3 of us) and we would always go and get some chips from the fish and chips shop afterwards, which I loved.

My mum would be at home, preparing the meals, seeing to the home, etc. She may well have been with us a lot of times, but I don't remember that happening so much. If she did, I feel she was more likely to watch than join in so to speak. She would be on the sidelines as opposed to getting stuck in with play. It never bothered me, at the time, but I think it is just something as I write this book that I recall.

I continued to feel unseen. Of course, I had been programmed into being unseen by the abuser. This was a normal way of life. I never understood any difference. Looking back, in order for him to feel in control, or more powerful than I, I was conditioned to feel that this was who I was meant to be. I felt beneath others and unimportant.

It's funny how much my brother made me feel like s**t, but I still looked up to him. He was my elder brother and I thought that meant something. I thought he would look after me. That is what big brothers do, isn't it? They look out for their younger siblings. Somewhere along the line, this is what I thought. Where I got that idea from, I do not know. It was as though it was an unconscious knowing. Why would I question that?

There are various memories again that have popped up over the years. He would always hurt me in some way. Whether it was a punch, a trip of the foot to make me fall. A pulling of the hair or...

One moment that would stick in my mind was when he was chasing me around the dining table at my home. I must have been around 9. My mum was in the kitchen with my dad and they were washing up or something. There was a window that looked out onto the kitchen in the dining room and there were double windows by the table at the end of the dining room which looked out to the garden. The top pane was clear glass and the bottom was frosted. He was chasing me around this table and I was shouting for him to leave me alone. As I had run around to get away from him, he had managed to trip me over. I lost my footing and plunged headfirst into the bottom window, **BANG**!!! The window cracked from my head going into it at full force.

My dad came rushing out of the kitchen and rather than checking if I was ok or telling my brother off for tripping me, it was me who got scolded and sent to my room, but not before being given a few hard smacks on my bottom. I cried my eyes out. I was upset. My head was throbbing, yet it was me who got punished.

How was that fair? What had I done to deserve that?

This was another occasion where I realised everything was my fault and no matter how much I spoke up, it would be *me* who would get into trouble.

That is what happens you see. If you are being ignored when you are suffering, you learn to deal with everything internally. I grew up knowing that no matter how much I was being hurt, no one would come to my rescue.

My cries continued to be unheard. Where was everyone? Why was I being ignored? I must deserve this then! This must be normal! It *is* my fault these things are happening to me.

Every time I try to reach out, the negative thoughts about myself are reinforced.

So the abuse continued.

I was subjected to name-calling, verbal abuse, the punching, the tripping, the pulling of the hair, the emotional blackmail… I remember many of the non-sexual assaults, but my brain has switched off beyond that and doesn't allow me to go to those parts.

Even now, I struggle to remember much about those aspects. I do remember numerous times kissing me and wanting penetration.

I remember the manipulation, disguising this as love.

I remember the secrecy around it.

The scare tactics of trying to get me to keep quiet.

The inappropriate touching.

My screams for help.

There were times when he did these things in plain sight.

How even when my parents were present there would be touching under a blanket or whilst they were in the room next door or when we would be made to sleep in the same bed if we had family staying over.

How the bed (my parent's bed) would be creaking when we were in there.

I remember one particular time when he was on top of me simulating having sex, again my memory has switched off as to whether there was actual penetration that night. My parents heard the bed making a noise and all they did was shout at us from downstairs and tell us to stop bouncing on the bed. I mean, for fuck's sake, the warning signs were there. How did they not realise something was going on? How???

I remember I must have only been about 9 or 10 years old, but I was lying on a camp bed in my bedroom (I think we had other kids staying the night before). I was lying in the sleeping bag and I was sobbing. I was distraught.

I had the sleeping bag zipped up over my head so no one could see or hear me. There and then, I wanted to end my life.

I'd had enough.

Whatever I was feeling I wanted it to stop.

I can even remember what I wore.

I had green khaki trousers on and I wore a belt around my waist to keep my trousers secure.

I managed to take the belt off of my trousers and put it around my neck. I tied it around me like a noose and I would tug at it, crying as I tightened it a little bit more as I pulled it in.

Did I want to kill myself?

I know I wanted the pain to go away.

The feeling of worthlessness and despair. I was at the end of my tether.

I just didn't know what to do to stop the pain.

I was a child and didn't really know *how* to do it. I just felt the pain continue, feeling lost and worthless.

I don't remember what happened after that. My brain has decompartmentalized a lot. The disclosure of what happened was too unbearable for me to comprehend, so I dissociated from it.

Eventually, this meant I learned to desensitise what was happening. I could pretend (to a point) that none of this was happening.

After all, I lived with the abuser. There was no escape. He was someone I was supposed to be able to trust. He was family.

So, I carried on. I knew I would never breathe a word of it again. (Not for a good number of years anyway).

My innocence was taken away from me. My life was panned out in a way that I could never imagine. From the age of around 6 years old, I suffered abuse on and off for almost 40 years. Cycles being repeated, each decade that went by, from one abuser to another. Each I thought would be my saviour, but instead were just the devils in disguise. The abuse reincarnated over and over within different guises.

# CHAPTER 4
# PATTERNS

I will move on to the time when I was around 12. By this time, as far as I remember, the abuse had stopped from 'abuser **1**' shall we call him. I believe this stopped because my periods started as I don't remember anything happening after that.

It was only then that I had the realisation that the things happening to me, were NOT normal. They should *not* have happened. They were wrong.

This left me really confused, I felt ashamed. Here I was, in a family where I felt isolated, but I still had an immense feeling of loyalty. Remember for 4 or 5 years or so, I had tried to tell someone, but it was unnoticed. It was ignored. *I* was ignored.

I hadn't been listened to, I felt like I didn't matter and my self-esteem was at an all-time low.

My school life was extremely difficult. I would sit at the back of the class and I would rarely put my hand up to ask or answer questions for fear of looking stupid or saying something wrong. Everyone at school and at home just thought I was shy. That was my nature they thought, not knowing what actually laid beneath the surface.

The scared little girl, keeping quiet to save the peace. To not cause waves. To go under the radar. This was my survival mechanism. My coping strategy. This was what I needed to be to get myself through *each minute, each hour, each day.*

I started secondary school. Still at this time, I had told no one. I did not breathe a word. I had managed to continue to dissociate the pain from the earlier years. This was common practice for me. I became numb to the pain. I was able to subconsciously put it all in the back of my mind. No one would believe me, right? So, what was the point in thinking about it?

It still hadn't totally hit me that what had happened was not normal. I knew it didn't feel right, or good, but I didn't understand how wrong it was.

I hadn't been taught how 'love 'should be as I had a distorted, warped reality of what it was through the abuse and emotional unavailability surrounding me.

It only started to dawn on me at 12 years old, when a girl in my year had disclosed sexual abuse to the teachers and it had got out to the pupils that this had happened. Suddenly I had been hit with the enormity of what had happened to me.

For the very first time, I had considered telling someone.

I remember thinking how brave she was to do that and as I am writing this, I wonder where she is now. Whether she has a good life and found her way. I pray she lived a life from thereon with happiness and support. I will probably never know, but I hope so. I hope it didn't affect her life as it did mine. Maybe one day she will read this and reach out. Who knows.

But, just as I was contemplating speaking up, ANOTHER pupil spoke up about HER abuse and hers appeared very similar to mine. **BANG.....** Suddenly, all those negative words came back into my consciousness. I resorted back to what had been drummed into me:

**'No one will believe you.'**

I feared that others would think I was getting on the bandwagon and be accused of making it up... It would be another 5 years until I would even dare think of telling someone again.

At 14 I started working on a Saturday at a clothes shop. It was owned by an Asian man, I would say he would have been in his late 40's, or 50's. His hair was thinning on top and combed over to the side. He was a short man, only around the same height as I was. He had a couple of other men working there also in the warehouse at the back of the shop.

I was still at school at that point, so it was just a little pocket money for me and my friend to earn, so we had a little money in our pockets to do the usual teenage stuff, buy clothes or a little bit of light make up. We earned a mere £10 per day, but at the time, it seemed like loads; even though looking back, you could work an hour for that now. But I would do a full 8 hours. It was a unisex clothes shop, mainly denim, from what I remember. The owner would *insist* that we wear items of clothing from the shop to serve customers in. We used to turn up in the shop and he would pick up the clothes we were to wear and we would be told to go into the shop's dressing rooms and get changed.

The job was short-lived, I can't remember how long we were there, but I feel it was only about 4 or 5 weekends or so, it may have been more. Until things started to take a turn.

When we would go into the changing rooms, the owners would spy on us and walk by, or loiter out in the back whilst we were in there. We knew this because there would always be a gap in the curtains at the side of the cubicle as it wouldn't quite fit to close the gap fully.

We would catch them walking by whilst we were undressing. At first, I hadn't realised what was happening, unsure if we could actually be seen, but as time went on, they would start to be more blatant and do other things. Brush up against us. Look us up and down seductively. Eventually they began to touch us inappropriately, trying to fondle our breasts. When this happened, I felt sick to my stomach. I left for the day and decided I was **never** going back there.

Being pulled into another vulnerable position against my will, by men exerting their power. People in a position of trust abusing kids, using control to inflict their warped sexual desires onto underage girls. We were 14 years old for fucks sake. What gives these men the right to violate children like this?

Here I was again, falling victim to another perpetrator. Patterns repeating.

I did not say a word. I told no-one.

In fact, this is the first time I have ever spoken about this.

My whole childhood had been taken over by abuse. This pattern was built, through no fault of my own. AGAIN, men are showing me that I am not important, my body is not my own. Wondering if this is normal for people to want to treat others like this or was it just to ME.

I *never* told my parents; I *never* told my friends.

Looking back, I didn't even speak about it with the friend who worked alongside me. It just shows how much manipulation was involved, feeling forced into keeping silent.

The cycle of abuse happened to me, yet I felt I couldn't tell.

How utterly sad is it that I was made to feel like that? I wonder how many other children have been put through this. Repeatedly being violated in every way. Feeling powerless to do anything about it. I know the statistics are shocking.

*Another* fucking secret I felt I had to keep to myself.

When I recall things like that, I realise just how many (not all) men treat women like objects. On occasions, I would walk home in the evenings on my own from my friends' houses (no more than around 10-15 minutes' walk) and the number of times I would see a car pull up at the side of the road, driving by the pavement slowly, men, yelling out to get my attention… All I was doing was minding my own business, trying to get home from my friends and there they were, looking for their next prey like I was some kind of prostitute.

Bizarrely, it almost felt normal. This may be partly the reason as to why I didn't tell anybody. All of this going on in my life and I kept silent, thinking this was just part of life.

The severity of the abuse I suffered has only really hit me over the last few years. It makes me really sad that this is how my early life formed. There must have been signs back home. I am sure of it. Being a parent myself now, I honestly can't fathom that there were no signs at all.

Even when I didn't turn up at work the following Saturday aged 14, I remember I was in bed and my dad brought up the house phone telling me there was a man on the other end, asking for me. I answered and told him I wasn't going back. I just don't recall my dad questioning me about it afterwards...

Now I am 15 years old. I guess you could say, I was just getting into 'boys' a little. They were starting to take a bit more interest in me. It was the usual thing, often, boys would try and annoy you because that meant they 'liked you', or so we are led to believe.

I mean how warped it is that society tells boys at a young age that a way to show you like a girl, is to annoy her or be mean in some way? For me this was not a new or unexpected thing, just another part of growing up, given my past. Boys always end up treating you a certain way when they say they like or love you don't they? That is what my childhood taught me.

When I was a teenager, we used to go to the fairground. Every September the fair would show up in Barking Park. My friends and I used to go there every night. We would love it. We would go on the waltzers and suchlike.

Considering I was so shy and introverted with people, I was (and still am) a bit of an adrenaline junkie. I loved all of the scarier rides. The big wheels, things that turn you upside down, rides that throw you up in the air. I did all sorts of stuff and the scarier the better, I loved them!

Me and my friend at the time liked these two boys and one of them ended up being my very first experience of a 'boyfriend.' I was 15 and he was 18. We were together for around a year, so it was a 'serious' relationship in our minds. I was head over heels with him, everything was great for a while but eventually, he became possessive over me and his behaviour started to unnerve me. I remember I was scared to end the relationship as I didn't know how he was going to react.

When I told him, he became very cross. He told me to get into his car. I did and he sped down the road like a bat out of hell. He threatened that he didn't want to live anymore if I left him, using emotional blackmail to try and persuade me to stay with him. But I didn't. This was the end. I was *not* going back.

This was the start of the spiral, meeting the wrong men. It just happened. It was not in any way a conscious decision. I didn't want a 'bad' boy. I guess it goes back to what I felt was familiar. Not cognitively but in my body. The chaos almost felt safe, even though, as time went on, this would prove to be highly dangerous.

My next relationship was when I was 17. My friends and I used to go to a local nightclub. It was back in the times when we used to have a slow dance right at the end of the evening (cringey I know). There was a guy there that I had seen down at the local pub close to where I lived. Me and my bestie Ang used to spend a lot of our time socialising there. Most of the people there were from my school, so I had grown up with people there. We had that tight-knit community where we all looked out for each other.

We ended up on a Saturday night down the nightclub. It was the end of the evening, around 2am and the slow dances came on. He asked me to dance and the rest was history.

We lived in each other's pockets from that day forward. Within about 3 months we knew we both wanted to be married. Have kids. Even to the point of deciding on what names we would call our children. We were smitten.

He was around 4 years older than I was. I had a year of the relationship with the possessive guy at 15, but this was *real*. This was the one! No doubt. We were swept up in all the romance of 'young love.'

Fast forward a couple of years, we decided to get our first home together. We spent a lot of time with his family. They were always together in those days. They spoke to each other every day. We met up with each other all the time. This was completely different to how I thought my family was.

At this time, it was what I had dreamed of my family life to be. This was the fairytale I had concocted in my head. This was how a family *should* be. Not the disoriented car crash of a family life in my mind I was used to. I put them all on a pedestal. My romantic notion of what I thought a family should be. The family my inner child craved!

At 18, we had ups and downs, due to my childhood. I found having a sexual relationship was difficult. Part of me enjoyed intimacy but every now and again, I wouldn't want it. I didn't really know why. It would just come and go. No known reason at the time as to why I would go off it. Obviously, I had a lot of unresolved trauma from the sexual abuse I had endured for most of my childhood and I was still living in silence.

Our relationship became a little difficult. I was going through a phase of not wanting intercourse. My partner was getting annoyed about it. I guess he took it as I wasn't so interested in him and he challenged me about it one day. Under pressure I blurted out what had happened to me. There was shock from both sides. There were tears from each of us. He made me tell him who had done it to me. I didn't want to. I still didn't speak about it enough to process it. We cried. But then it was like we had an unwritten rule that we would never mention it again. We didn't.

Eventually our relationship got back on track again and we just continued getting on with our lives. As *'normal'* as that could be.

We decided that we were going to live together and took steps to make it happen. I was 20 at this point.

He always liked a flutter on the horses. His dad was into betting, especially the races. To me, this was a hobby. Nothing serious, just a little flutter on a Saturday afternoon. My boyfriend popped down the bookies to place a bet. None of my family did anything like that, so I never really got the fascination, but hey... that is what he was into, so who am I to judge it in any way?

He worked in London and he and I worked in the same workplace for a while, but eventually I started working in Dagenham for a Health and Safety department. We had just bought our first house together, so we were 'living the dream.' We barely argued in this relationship and it was just like we were 'loves young dream.'

We didn't have a joint bank account at that time, so the bills came out of his bank account and every payday he would pick me up to take me to the bank to get my share of the bills out. I would give him around £500 per month to go towards bills and food etc. In those days, I didn't earn very much, so this was more than half of my month's wages. But I would go in and take the money out and hand it to him, no questions asked.

We had always wanted to have children. We decided to get married and when he proposed I was over the moon. I felt like a princess. He asked me at his parent's house upstairs in one of the bedrooms. He had written a lovely little card telling me how much he loved me. I loved words. At that time, I believed everything I was being told. I think because I was desperately wanting the fairytale ending.

Planning the wedding was a bit of a stressful time. As most weddings are, but this felt on another level because neither side of the families particularly got on. This made things quite awkward and there were many times I asked myself "Why am I doing this?".

There were arguments. There was pressure to do everything for everyone else.

It was *our* wedding, no one else's, but it didn't feel that way. I remember on the wedding day, my father was giving me away. We got to the church and I remember getting out of the wedding car and my dad turned to me and told me if I wasn't sure I didn't have to go through with it. I'll be honest, at that moment, I did feel a little apprehensive, but I put that down to jitters so shrugged it off and carried on down to the church. I hated any kind of spotlight on me, so having to walk down the aisle with all these eyes on me felt really overwhelming, but I got through it. The service was super long. Being a Catholic family, this is what they were like. So many hymns and prayers were read out. It seemed to go on for ages. But we had done it! We were now Mr. and Mrs.

We were going to Ibiza for our honeymoon. We had decided very early on that as soon as we got married, we would try for a baby. My need for my own family was so important to me. I wanted to have my own to give them the happy childhood that I didn't have.

# CHAPTER 5
# LOSS

I was 21 when we got hitched. It wasn't unusual to be married that young. It was just what happened. We got to the honeymoon and I felt a little rough. I hadn't realised until we got there, but I had fallen pregnant. We were so shocked, but both of us were thrilled. This is what we had BOTH wanted so much. What we had spoken of constantly. Sadly, when we had literally just found out I was pregnant the joy of pregnancy was short-lived. No sooner had we found out we were pregnant, I started to bleed. We were devastated, heartbroken.

What had we done to deserve this? The one thing that I wanted so badly; to have a family I could be a part of and care for wholeheartedly, was taken away from us. We had only known for a few days, but we were invested.

A short time went by and I fell pregnant again for the second time.

Overjoyed, I couldn't wait for us to be a family. Having a miscarriage the first time around meant we were so happy, but anxious given what happened last time. I would have been around 9 weeks pregnant the second time. Overwhelming sadness came back into our lives. We sadly lost that baby too. We were distraught. All sorts of things were going on in my mind. Maybe I couldn't carry children. Maybe my past was a punishment. Maybe this is never going to happen, I thought. A second time, literally finding out but it was whisked away from us almost instantly. The emotional rollercoaster at its harshest.

I took it that it was my fault. There must be something wrong with me. I can't even house a baby in my belly sufficiently enough for it to survive, the feelings of failure crept in.

The one thing I wanted so badly was not going to happen to me. I felt my chances of being a mum were very slim. I thought time would be running out. It was strange how I felt that time would be running out for me to have a baby as at this time I was only around 22 years old, but I think looking back, my need to have a family took over my emotions. In my mind, this would be my chance to undo all the hurt I had suffered as a child. I would be able to rewrite history. Make my child happy and be a good mum to him/her.

Babies were all around me at that time too, which I think was a big factor in me wanting a family so urgently. One of his sisters had just had a baby when I lost my second one and this was really hard for me to take in. She hadn't even planned to have a baby. Although she was loved when she was born, she really didn't want to have one. She already had 2 and kept saying that she definitely didn't want another. But she had one.

I felt angry, I wanted one so badly yet I ended up losing mine. I felt cheated and it was heartbreaking.

I had to have a 'D&C' after the second miscarriage. I hadn't been offered one with the first. Because it happened when I was abroad, I came home and went to the Doctors, and it felt like they dismissed the miscarriage even existed. I felt angry about that because no matter how quickly it had gone, he or she was very much a part of me. This time, I was put out in general anaesthetic and once the procedure was done, the baby was no longer there. I remember afterwards, the pain in my lower belly. The constant reminder of our loss.

We continued to try after I had healed a bit more. Fast forward a year later and I fell pregnant. I was overjoyed. I was crying with happiness but also fearful in case it may be another that couldn't go full term. I was wishing time away in the early stages. Constantly going to the toilet to check I hadn't lost it. Praying I was not going to find some blood there. It took away a little of the joy for a while. Every time I had a pain in my belly, I would panic that it was happening all over again. I got to around 9 weeks, the furthest I had been in terms of pregnancy, but I was still unable to completely relax.

Shortly afterwards, at the 9-week stage, I got a letter for my 12-week scan.

At this point I had started getting terrible morning sickness. I would be at work and would finish at around 4.30pm. Every day without fail, at 4pm I would feel sick. I would have to rush down to the toilets to throw up in the cubicle. It was like clockwork. This would then continue until 10.30 in the evening. I would be fine one minute and then bang, I would feel sick. I'd rush to the toilet and throw up bile. I would get ready for bed and I would go to brush my teeth and of course, this would be my last chuck up of the night!

My husband had always wanted children as much as I did. We had talked about it so much in our relationship. Remember, we were only a few months into our relationship and decided on their names. Not at any point did I wonder if this was not the case. Not at any point did I doubt that.

But as the pregnancy went on, he became more and more distant. He had many nieces and nephews and he was always gushing over them. I remember when his sister was pregnant, he would often go up to her and feel her belly as her baby would move. A foot here, an arm there poking out and he would be straight over there, wanting to feel her moving. I had no worries at all that he was going to be a fantastic dad.

But suddenly, he wasn't like that with me.

He started to be less interested in me. As time went on this became more and more apparent.

I was confused and didn't understand. Things started to change within him.

Eventually our daughter was born. I was overjoyed, she came really quickly in the end. I had literally finished work on the Friday to go on maternity leave, thinking I would have at least a couple of weeks to get things together before the baby arrived. As she wasn't due until the 8th of the month and being my first full-term baby, I just took it as standard that our baby would be late. But no. Finished work on Friday. Went into labour first thing Monday morning.

I woke up Monday morning around 6am with excruciating pains all around my back and the lower part of my bottom. I had thought that when I went into labour, I would feel it around my belly, so when it was around the back, I thought I had terrible constipation.

I sat on the toilet for probably about an hour or so. I was making all sorts of noises and my husband stayed in bed. I remember feeling pissed off that he was just letting me get on with it - he was only in the other room with the door open. In the end, I had to shout for him as the pain was progressing quite rapidly. He got on the phone to the midwife who asked how quickly the contractions were coming. By then I couldn't distinguish between when the pain started and when it ended as they were coming in thick and fast. He shouted that I needed to go to the hospital. There I was, walking around whilst having contractions, picking up my hospital bag and anything else I might need to take with me. We got into the car, as they had said that it would be quicker in our car than it would be to wait for an ambulance.

I remember the journey, I was yelling in pain and had overwhelming urges to push. It felt like the longest journey of our lives. We got to the doors of the hospital and by this time I could barely walk. Luckily there was someone by the door who saw us coming and they managed to grab a wheelchair for me before I collapsed in a heap on the floor.

I was taken up to the labour ward. I had gone into the room where the midwife asked me to go to the toilet to take a sample.

I took the little container with me, but I was in full-blown labour. There was no way I could pee in this little tube as all I wanted to do was push. I shouted out to the nurse and they came running in and got me on the bed. I was already 10cms dilated. She was on her way.

My husband nearly missed it. Rather than wanting to be by my side like I needed him to be, he was more interested in running outside to call his family. The midwife stopped him and sternly told him if you leave now, you are going to miss it. She was on her way.

By 10:29am she was born. No time for any pain relief whatsoever. Not even gas and air.

Amazing how the pain just seems to disappear once the little bundle of joy arrives and is placed in your arms.

Finally, we had our little family. We had a beautiful little girl. It was the most magical moment of my life. It felt like it had taken a lot of time for us to get there, but we had done it. This little bundle of joy was going to make us complete.

The first few weeks we had lots of visitors, everyone loved to come and see our little girl. She was so loved.

The novelty had started to wear off as my husband wasn't helping very much.

He became doting when his family were about, or we had other visitors. But when it was just the 2 of us, he wouldn't really do too much at all. I continued to feel confused.

I was absolutely knackered. The first 10 weeks I was getting next to no sleep. Visitors had started to slow down like they do. He went back to work after a few weeks. He would work shifts, so he was out at all times of the day and night. He would work more. He wouldn't really be present. Night times were hard because I wasn't getting any respite. I remember he was home one Saturday and he wanted to go and look at a car in a showroom with his parents and one of his sisters. I had to feed our daughter and being a new mum, I was still getting used to the routine. He wanted to be in London at a certain time and got really angry with me as I was taking too long to get the baby fed and ready in time. All he did was have a go at me and make me feel like shit, telling me that his sister would be ready on time when her daughter was younger. He'd say I was a crap mum and if she can do it, why can't I.

The baby was bottle-fed, so what he could have done was bloody help me. But no. He couldn't do that, it was down to *me*. By this time, I was in tears. We eventually got out of the door. Drove over and we turned up at this showroom. It was obvious to everyone I had been crying. His mother and sister came up to me asking what was wrong. I told them and they told me to ignore him. We spent a lot of time with his family. Given the family dynamic with mine, this to me felt how it should be. They wanted to spend time together, whereas in my family it always felt forced and out of having to, rather than wanting to.

Every time my parents came over, I barely had any food in the house. My husband would give me minimal money for essentials. They would come over and I hadn't even had any milk in the house for a cup of tea. I didn't work at this time as I had our daughter to look after. I absolutely hated the fact that I had to ask for money. I have noticed this has been another pattern in my life. I hated having to ask anyone to help me. **Even** with things like that. I never felt comfortable asking for anything or being beholden to anyone. Let's face it, I had lived all through my life coping with things in silence, so looking back, it wasn't surprising I struggled with this later in life.

He would sometimes get up early when he was on days and I could hear him tearing up paper. I thought it was a little odd, but despite the red flags, I trusted him and I believed him when he told me there was nothing wrong. He did tell the odd white lies here and there. I still thought that overall he would be honest with me.

I will give you an example of the little things I mean. He smoked and his family didn't know about it. He was the only smoker in the family. I went through a phase of smoking, but I gave up as soon as we wanted to have children. I was never a heavy smoker anyway, so for me I didn't find it too difficult to stop. He would lie about it to me. I knew he was still smoking; I could smell it on him for goodness sake, but he would gaslight me trying to make me think I was making it up and imagining it all.

One night, it had gotten dark and he said he was popping outside. I looked out the window to see what he was doing and I literally could see him throw the butt over the fence at the front of the house. The lit fag end was glowing a bright red and I could see it fly out of his hand and into the air towards the outside gate leading to the road. He walked in, stinking of nicotine and I told him I had watched him throw the butt across the front garden. He looked me in the eye and lied to my face. This should've been a sign of things to come, but to me, it wasn't too important in the scheme of things. I was quite lighthearted about it, even though I was miffed that he had tried to make out I was imagining it.

Time went on and when our daughter was around 3 months old, it was suggested we move. We wanted to get a bigger place as we had outgrown our current home. We looked around various properties and came across a newspaper article. New houses were being built in an area in Essex. We had never been there before, nor heard of it, but different from Dagenham, the prices were so low and affordable, so we decided to have a look.

In those days we only had to put a £5000 deposit to secure the property, so we decided this was the property we wanted and bought off plan. We found the deposit and over the next 6 months watched our home being built.

My husband wanted to take control of all the finances for the house move. He knew a lady who was a financial advisor for the company he worked for. I did meet her, but he was very adamant that he went to the meetings alone to discuss mortgages etc. Not wanting to bother me with the fine details as I had a lot on my plate with our daughter. He didn't feel I needed to be there. My nose was a little put out of joint as I wanted to be a part of the whole process, but I didn't really question it. Mum duties were calling, so I just accepted it.

We would visit the property and see it taking shape. It was so exciting to buy something with just seeing plans, rather than the finished article, and so we were very excited.

Moving day finally arrived. The property was beautiful. We managed to get some furniture in. It had a generous-sized garden. Perfect for our little family to grow. My husband was working more and more and with the journey being a bit longer for him, it wasn't unusual for him to be in bed for quite a while during the day so I would get up and get our daughter ready. He would go straight to work until the early hours again, so we never spent a huge amount of time together on the face of it.

# CHAPTER 6
# RED LETTER DAY

I started to hear him tearing up paper when the postman arrived. By this time it was clear something was up. One day, I decided to search where these letters were from. I opened up the bin and there were ripped-in-half red letters staring back at me.

This was the start of it unfolding. Realising the amount of debt he had got us into. By this time, we were in our new house. I realised that we were in trouble. I remembered the times when he would pick me up from work and take my money to 'pay the bills.' I realised he had been moving my money to fund his gambling habit. The more I delved into the backlog of statements, I could see all the extent of what he was spending it on.

I confided in one of my oldest friends. I met her when I worked in London. I had been made redundant and was given a job in Stratford. We became firm friends and did lots together over the years, she quickly became an addition to my family, as I had hers. She has been one of my closest friends for nearly 30 years.

She came over to help me piece it all together one day when he was at work. We had gone through all the bank statements I could find. We found he had got us into debt for over £30,000. I was devastated. I hadn't realised that he was into gambling as much as he was as he had hidden so much from me.

I decided to confront him.

He was in bed; I had got up with our daughter and she had fallen asleep in the lounge.

I walked into our bedroom. I had the statements in hand.

He went as *white* as a sheet. He turned over onto his front and buried his head in his pillow. He couldn't look at me. He knew he had been well and truly busted.

I said my piece and I went back downstairs and waited for him to get up. I wanted him to explain himself, but he did not want to talk. He refused, saying he didn't have time. He got up and went to work again to avoid further confrontation.

What was I going to do? What was HE going to do? I had no clue, but we needed to get out of this. We needed to get our finances back on track, but he was in denial.

There we were, with a baby under 1. In debt. I wasn't working as I was looking after our daughter. I couldn't contribute money-wise. But we needed to do something. I felt totally blindsided. My trust had been blown. I couldn't believe he could lie to me like that and have *nothing* to say in his defence. I felt totally destroyed.

But he was still my husband. I did not want our family to fall apart.

'Till Death Us Do Part' and all that!

The last thing I wanted was to split up the family because of this. Ironic isn't it. That statement alone showed how I felt it was my problem to solve. The ownness of me to fix things. Me to hold everything and everyone together. The patterns emerging yet again. More people pleasing. I had been hurt and betrayed in so many ways, but it was me who felt the guilt and shame of his actions. My heart was heavy. I had to be strong.

I decided that we needed to get back on track. We had a daughter together. We said our vows. 'For better or for worse'. I did not want to give up.

I still loved him and cared for him deeply. I didn't at that point feel I couldn't fight for our marriage. Having a broken home was not an option. I did not want this for my daughter.

I spoke to him about getting some help with his gambling problems. I don't remember him being particularly resistant to this at the time, but I wasn't totally convinced that he was completely on board either. But he agreed. I looked into a help group, which was Gamblers Anonymous. I found one in our local area and he agreed to go. I drove him there to support him and I said I would wait for him in the car until he had finished. I think the session was around an hour or so. I could see him from the car as the building it was held in had quite a lot of windows. I remember feeling relieved that he had agreed to go along and prayed that this was the start of us getting our lives back together.

Time had passed over the next few months, he stuck to the weekly meetings. I was so proud of him. He seemed proud of himself too. He clearly got something out of it and was reaping the benefits.

Time passed. We seemed to be getting back on track. He even invited me to a meeting where family could attend, to see what goes on within a session and to celebrate the people there and their achievements. Things looked like they were on the up. Finally...

Our home was beautiful. It was a lovely little cul-de-sac. Perfect for us. A lovely field in front of our front garden. We were semi-detached, but we were at the end home on our road. The other house attached was on a different road, which we thought was cool at the time. Compared to our previous home, it was like a palace. A lovely decent-sized garden for our daughter to play in. We were about an hour away from family and friends on both sides, but it looked like a positive move for both of us.

Things were going well for a while. But, as time went on, things started to go downhill. We never had a lot of time together as a family. He was becoming distant.

He was spending a longer time away. Going to work earlier. Coming home later.

He would tell me it was because he was attending GA meetings and he would need to leave early to go to them, going on to work after. Or vice versa. Attend the GA meetings after he had finished work. This continued for quite a while. But as time went on the explanations got harder to believe. I became suspicious. The stories he was telling me just didn't ring true. It became clear he was lying.

I started to ask questions.

These questions were not received particularly well so the mask started to drop. He would get annoyed at me for asking him questions. Still insisted he was attending GA. I would ask him for information about the meetings he was attending. He would be travelling to far-away meetings. It just didn't ring true anymore. As time went on, my gut instinct was that he wasn't being honest with me. He was lying to me. Here we go again.

I told him I was losing trust in him and I would rather he be honest, no matter what the answers were. My view was that an answer I didn't want to hear was still better than a lie. So, I called his bluff. I told him that I wanted him to take me to another meeting, like he did before. You could see him squirming. His face as he was trying to think of an excuse that sounded feasible enough to prevent me from attending. But I was done with his lies. I wasn't going to be swayed to leave it, so I pursued.

Eventually he ran out of reasons and used the last one he could think of which was, we could not get a babysitter for the meeting. Original huh! Giving no choice but to have to go on his own.

Determined to get to the truth, I was not going to stop with that.

After all, I really wanted us to work on this and get through it. I didn't want us to lose each other in all of this. I was fighting for us to work. I ended up speaking to his mother and she agreed to have our daughter for a few hours while we went.

You could see the sweat particles forming on his face. He was panicking. He knew now that he was going to be found out. That I was going to work out that he had NOT been attending any of the meetings he said he had. Which he had lied to my face about. He had continued to lie and get us into more chaos.

I had given him chance after chance, but it was just more lies. That was the hardest part of it all. It got to the stage where I couldn't trust anything he said anymore. Eventually we stopped sleeping in the same room. We grew apart significantly. We were barely talking by this point. He continued to be away from home. I was practically a single mum. I did everything for our daughter on my own. I felt sad. This was someone I was going to be with forever. I ached for a forever family. The one I had always dreamed of having. But it was never going to happen.

Our relationship was non-existent. Separate sleeping arrangements continued. To be honest, we were already over, but I was in denial. Gambling was more important to him; he was an addict. The urge to gamble became greater than the family. Us or the bookies. The bookies won.

Inevitably, we split up. He got up one morning and he just left. He didn't tell me where he was going. For the sake of our daughter, I spoke to his eldest sister and it turned out he was staying with her. I asked her why he hadn't been in touch with me to see his daughter and she said she didn't know.

He did not show interest in our daughter. He would often say he was coming to take her out. To spend some time with her, but he either wouldn't show up or he would cancel at the last minute. He would just text me late the night before. He was due to have her for a couple of hours but was consistently letting her down.

He wasn't contributing towards me in any way of maintenance, so I was struggling.

I needed to work but looked after our daughter 24/7 on my own. I needed to put food on our table and cover the bills. It was bloody hard.

I would ask him for some help and he would give me a little. Telling me he would pay me 'x' amount but would only give me half of that amount, or nothing at all. He would try to tell me he would pay it on another date. But all I would hear is the same old excuses. Same old story, time and time again.

I told him if he didn't help out with his daughter, I would have no choice but to go to the CSA as it was called then. It was clear he did not want me to do that. He worked for a good company and earned a decent amount of money per month. But of course, he needed to have this to fund his gambling addiction. He did *not* want to give me any. His priorities were for himself, not putting food on his daughter's table.

In his mind, he wasn't living with us, so why should he pay? That was his mindset and this continued throughout ALL my daughters' childhood. I received nothing for so long. Occasionally CSA would catch up with him and take some from his employer in dribs and drabs. Then he would leave that job and dodge CSA by accepting cash in hand (presumably). He had friends who were in high places within this company and it appeared that they were covering up for him in order to help him dodge the CSA. He did this for many, many years. I struggled so much because of this. The financial effect on myself and our daughter was awful.

But I had no choice but to work it out. I had spent all my life 'just working it out'.

Surviving, never thriving. Tired, I ended up getting a job working nights. One of my neighbours who I became friends with would share a job. My daughter would wake up in the night wanting to be in my bed to sleep. But I couldn't have her with me because the phone could go at any moment. I was permanently exhausted. No help from him or his family.

I had always left the door open for his family. His mum and dad had literally moved down the road from where we had lived. I had always (so I thought) had a fantastic relationship with them. I always wanted them in our daughter's life, so I always told them they could visit any time.

They never did.

I never saw them again.

They washed their hands of us. Never knew why. Still don't.

Blood is thicker than water I suppose. They would cover for him. They would turn a blind eye to what he was doing. More to the point, *not* doing, for our daughter. They enabled him to have no accountability as a parent.

I do remember talking to one of his sisters once during this time. Having her brother spend a couple of years constantly dodging the CSA saying he wasn't at work, during a conversation, she let slip that he was working. Of course I hadn't doubted it all this time, but she said the words right out of her mouth. I quizzed her about this but she had realised her mistake so quickly tried to backtrack and wouldn't give me any information at all on him. That was the last I heard from her for quite a while. None of the family contacted me again, until a much later date.

My daughter and I continued to struggle with the day-to-day stresses. By this time, she had no relationship with her father. He had wiped his hands of her and carried on doing what he was doing. Seemingly without regrets. We had divorced by then. I was mortified that my marriage had ended but knew I had to just get on with it. I had no choice.

I was away from the area where I had grown up but I was lucky in many ways, as my daughter was in nursery school. I had made quite a few friends in the area. I had an outlet, where I could be around other women with young children. I felt like I had some support if I needed it. It was then I realised how important it was to have good friends around you.

In the relationship with my ex-husband, we had been quite insular. It had only really been us. When it had been good, we were very much in love. I couldn't keep dwelling on the past, I had to move on. You have to. As a parent, you have to find a way, you push through. I am a mum; I need to make sure my daughter is cared for in the way she deserves.

I had a few years again on my own. My daughter was coming to the end of her nursery years, getting ready to transition into junior school. It was a few days before the end of term, it was a big moment for myself and my daughter. I started talking to this woman. My daughter had one particular friend at nursery and she always used to talk to her, but I didn't know who her mum was. On the last day of nursery, we got chatting and then she and her daughter spent ALL summer with us and built up a friendship.

I had been on my own for a few years by this point and she kept speaking about her brother and would get us to pop in to see him, near where he lived. When I met him, I didn't really fancy him, to be honest. I wasn't really looking for a relationship, but my new friend kept organising these 'chance' meetings. I don't really know how it happened, but we ended up going on a few dates and things developed from there. He was different to what I would say I would be attracted to. I only had one really serious boyfriend and I married him, so I went in with an open mind.

# CHAPTER 7
# THE DEVIL IN DISGUISE

He was quite loud, not what I was used to. He was very sure of himself and I guess I was quite attracted to that. He could be quite outspoken but I guess in a way, that made me trust him. I felt I knew where I stood with him. He could be quite funny too at times.

He appeared to have quite a lot of friends when we first met, I was attracted to this as to me, that meant he must be a good person because he had people around him. His mum lived with him in his house at the time. He said he had split up from a long-term partner and his mum had helped him buy the ex out so he could continue to live there.

He seemed to have a good relationship with his mother, which I read as positive. I thought he must be caring as it sounded like she doted on him in many ways. I don't think I ever really thought I would be with him long-term because I hadn't really been looking for anyone when we met. I suppose I was just going with the flow and seeing where it took us. I wasn't considering any long-term plans.

Time went on and somehow things got more serious. I seemed to get swept away with it.

He and his family had met my daughter, because she and his niece were best friends from nursery school, so it seemed like a natural progression.

Looking back, there were many red flags, but I hadn't been educated. I didn't even know what red flags were. I was still only about 26/27 at that point and quite naïve of relationships. I never had clear role models to show me what a healthy relationship looked like. My parents were not really a unit. They weren't affectionate and were quite distant towards each other. That was how I remember it anyway. They may beg to differ.

This man wasn't like that with me. He was very affectionate and would always want to see me. He did a lot with his friends. He had a bit of a past, but again he was quite open about it, so in a way, I was in awe of his bluntness, possibly wishing I was a bit like that.

I never wanted to upset anyone and there he was, not giving a shit who he upset by speaking his truth. Maybe if I were a bit more like that, people wouldn't treat me in the way they have. If I were a bit more assertive.

Time went on and by this time he had moved in with me and my daughter. He was good with my daughter and they became really close. I was pleased. She didn't have a male role model as her dad didn't give a toss, so I was happy they seemed to be developing some form of a relationship.

He seemed to put me on a pedestal almost. As time went on, this was becoming difficult. I am human, I am going to make a mistake here and there, but when I would remind him that I wasn't bloody perfect, he would make me feel bad. I would feel a lot of pressure to be the perfect partner. People pleasing appeared again. Whatever was happening in my life, I would always look at myself first to see what I had done to make him upset with me.

We had been living in my home for a couple of years when I fell pregnant with my son. By this time, I was 31. The controlling tendencies started coming quicker into the relationship.

His mother had moved into the house behind my back garden. He even put a gate in the back fence so his mother could pop over to ours easily without having to walk around the block to get to us. This was ok at first, but in the end, she would just turn up and so would his sister, who at that point had become jealous of mine and her brother's relationship. We had worked at the same caring company, so we had mutual colleagues and clients. She had struck up a shit storm trying to meddle in our relationship over recent times and I would hear all sorts of nasty things being said. Mostly about her brother, but some would be aimed at me too. They would walk into our house like it was their own, which would cause a bit of tension as I felt my house was not our own anymore.

He became extremely critical of me in that he would want to do something and if I didn't want to, he would say things to make me feel bad. He would make a show of me in front of his family and I would feel like an idiot.

I recall I was around 6 months pregnant and he had decided just before I became pregnant that he didn't want the house the way it was because it was a house I had once shared with my ex-husband. We hadn't been in the house together that long considering. But he was insistent that he had to have it altered, rather than move so he suggested we extend. That way it would feel like it was 'our' house and not just mine.

I kind of understood his point, so I accepted. But while I was in my second trimester, we had our new kitchen fitted. He wanted it to all be done. I had felt sick throughout most of my pregnancy with our son and was quite big by this point. He wanted the cooker hood to be fitted and needed my help to put it up. I was exhausted as I was helping in every way I could with the new build as I wasn't allowed to take it easy. Pregnancy or not, that wasn't an option. If he had to do some work, there was no way I was sitting on my laurels.

He insisted on me helping him lift up the cooker hood so he could drill it into the wall. I said I couldn't lift something that heavy because of the baby but he wasn't having any of it. He made me lift it up for him! Whilst standing on a stall! Heavily pregnant with our child! I was in disbelief. He just couldn't wait until the morning to get someone else to help. He was putting our child at risk for a fucking cooker hood. I had streams of tears running down my face. I had already lost 2 babies in my 20's. I'd had a scare at 5 months this time around too, where I was bleeding. But I wasn't going to be let off the hook. He didn't give a shit. His focus was the kitchen. Not mine or our baby's health. His mum came in at the tail end of it and didn't say a word. Just watched in silence as tears rolled down my face.

He would often compare me to other women. He loved the thought of me being jealous. Making me feel insecure. I had never been a jealous type, but he would do all he could to make me feel inferior in order to make himself feel better.

He hated the fact that people liked me. He used to sarcastically say "Everyone likes you", like this was a negative thing. He was the jealous one, so instead he had to make me jealous.

He would be flirty with some of the other girlfriends or wives of his friends. He would go on at least 2 'lad's' holidays a year, one being Maguluf. He would openly talk about the women who would be there. It was the same women there every year. They all went on the same dates. His taunts to make me jealous even stretched to women on the TV. Constantly trying to make me feel ugly, or too fat or just not enough. His eyes were turning all the time and if I showed even a little that it was hurting me, he would do it even more.

He would put me down in order to make himself feel superior, all the while knocking my confidence and who I was as a person. His sister would always get on the bandwagon too.

She loved it when he put me down, because she had this strange relationship with him where she always wanted to seek approval from him. Looking back, I can see the pattern that she also felt inferior around him and considered herself the black sheep of the family. Their dad had passed away before I met them therefore, my partner was seen as the 'head of the family.' The dynamic was quite strange because both his sister and his mum had him on a pedestal. Whatever he said or did, they would back him. Turn a blind eye to his antics.

Our son had arrived by this point. He had arrived on the exact date we were given at our first scan. It was the day of Wimbledon and the Euros final. My partner had joked the baby MUST arrive in between both, so he didn't miss any of the tournaments. I remember rocking on one of those blow-up exercise balls to try to start labour by rocking on it. Never dreamed it would have worked! I had started dinner at 5pm that Sunday and I was in the middle of cooking a roast when my waters had broken. I hadn't experienced that with my daughter as they had to do that manually for me with her. What a weird sensation that is!

He was born at home, dead on 6pm, in between the tournaments!

I was only in labour for 60 minutes, the midwife only just arrived on time. No time for the other to get there, no time for any sort of pain relief. She had to do it herself. The pain was excruciating. Much worse than I remember with my daughter. But our son came into the world, healthy and gorgeous.

After he was born, my partner started looking into buying houses. To be honest, I loved the house we were in. I had just given birth in our home, but his mother was spending more and more time at our house and less time on her own. He had come up with the idea of selling both my house and his mother's house to buy a bigger home for us, but also for his mum to move with us. She was becoming more and more reliant on him as she was getting older. She became more dependent on him *and* us, to look after her. I ended up doing more for her than he did half the time.

If he had been out at work all day, he wouldn't come home and help. Another child to feed and I only had our son a few months ago, but I didn't have a long maternity leave. I felt pressure to work, so I was childminding other people's kids within a few weeks of having him. I also worked at a school in the kitchen at lunchtimes. If there was a knock at the door, I would be feeding the baby and he would be in the office by the front door but would rarely answer. I would have to get up with the baby whilst feeding him (I breastfed at that point) and I would go and answer the door. He would finish work early most days but would not help with our son. I had two jobs and still had to do all the school runs for my eldest trying to juggle feeds, keep the home. He would never help out, he didn't feel it was his role!

We eventually moved to the house with an annex and the house needed a lot of work. We did most of it ourselves. We converted the garage into an annexe for his mother.

# CHAPTER 8
# ISOLATION

I even worked 3 jobs at one point and this still wasn't good enough. He would say he loved me every day, but he was very opinionated. *Everything* I did was never enough. There was no way I could maintain his expectations. He lived an almost separate life to me. I was expected to be at home, looking after the kids predominantly but also expected to contribute financially to the family home. I was the cleaner. The cook. The partner. The mother. The supporter. The decorator. I was a doormat.

He had holidays with the lads. He'd spend thousands of pounds on his golfing hobbies. Every weekend he would be golfing. I was expected not to do anything. If I did, he would make me feel guilty. I was 'allowed' ONCE throughout our 10-year relationship to go on a mini break without him. But only when I was 6 months pregnant. I had no boundary-setting skills. In my mind, should I worry if he would do anything behind my back? When he is being so honest about it?

In my head, it was telling me that I could trust him. Sounds ridiculous now when I look back. Just because he had told me about his philandering past, as far as I was concerned, it wouldn't happen to me.

When we moved to the new house I had to do just as much manual work as he did, otherwise I would be accused of being lazy, or not wanting it enough. I was on constant eggshells and became a total walkover. I had so many insecurities and a lack of self-worth about who I was that I would accept anything. The bare minimum. I had to be this big achiever in our relationship, or I wasn't worthy. I had to step up to the mark in every aspect, or I would feel like a failure. I was a puppet. Having my strings pulled in every which way to get the breadcrumbs of love that I so craved.

When I look back, I can see just how sad my life has been. I was all over the place when it came to the men in my life. When I relate this back to my childhood, I can see more patterns. Truly I stood on eggshells as a child too. For one, I never knew when the abuser would strike, but also my dad, although he did a lot at weekends with me and my brother, he was the one out of my parents where we didn't want to step a foot wrong. To a point, I felt that I was frightened of getting on his wrong side. Don't get me wrong, I didn't feel scared of him on a day-to-day basis, he didn't do anything to make me frightened necessarily, but he *was* always the one who made all the decisions. Mum would shout and scream, but it was he who we would behave for more so. So the pattern had been there from my earliest years. I have only just realised this at this moment while writing.

Going back to my partner, the patterns were continuing. In different ways, but they were there. I constantly would think about what I did and what I said, 3 seconds before I did it. Imagine living a life like that. How draining and demoralising it was. How exhausting my life was. Perceiving danger every step of the way before it happened.

He would sometimes let me go out with friends (I made quite a few friends when we moved to the larger house with his mother). Notice I said he 'let' me. But he would either give me some grief about it before I left the house, putting a downer on the night out, or he would make me pay for it after.

He never physically hurt me, but he was very controlling and had a way of making me feel bad if I did anything without him, unless of course it benefited him in some way. I never really drank in my early adulthood. When I met this new group of friends from my children's school, I would start to enjoy the odd glass of wine. I hadn’t been a big drinker, the only thing I would drink was mainly spirits initially and even this was very rare. I would go out at this point and yes, I would enjoy myself and be a bit merry, but so was everyone else. The same if I went out with my partner. But he would make me feel bad about it. This escalated and he would gaslight me into thinking I did or said something bad whilst I was out. He said I made a show of him. A show of myself.

I would feel tremendous guilt and shame, because I thought I must have done and said these things, even though I didn’t remember it at all. I would be disgusted with myself, thinking I must have offended people I was out with. Of course, I started to limit my drinking on a night out. I would hold back when I met my friends. I wouldn’t go out every time I was asked, for fear that he would be annoyed at me, or I would do something stupid.

A few years later, when I spoke with my best friend, she was shocked, because I loved everyone when I had a few. I am happy, I am funny. More outgoing and she really shone a light on the fact that it was him making it appear that it wasn’t the case. To prevent me from fully enjoying an evening without him. Stopping me from going out altogether.

What was good for him, was definitely not good for me. We were on two different levels, as far as he was concerned. He was king of the castle and he wanted me to be the little woman, seen and not heard, whilst he led his best life. He had the best of both worlds.

Everyone used to say that he was punching when he got with me (a term when someone has a partner who is much better looking). His ego hated that, but equally liked that friends thought I was pretty. He was very much of the view that he had to be with someone who looked good, because that meant that he looked good. Other men would be in awe of him because it looked like he had everything. He is very materialistic too and although he was on a very modest wage, he would use what his women had to get up the ladder.

If they are useful to him, he will move all the stops to get what he wants. This meant that others would perceive him as a money earner. The alpha male. He could be quite obnoxious with it and this meant that although on the outside it looked like he had a lot of friends, they were all superficial. Many acquaintances. I'll scratch your back if you scratch mine. What can this person do for me? As much as some people liked him, there were more that didn't. They thought he was arrogant and mouthy. Which he was. He realised he was very insecure. He was masking that to the outside world, because this would have made him feel weak. Of course he was weak. If he must belittle others to make himself feel good, then there are definite insecurities and lack of self-worth in there. He had to dim my light to make him shine brighter. To make me not feel good enough and it did exactly that. He hated that I had made my own friends. When I had left my ex-husband, I had a very small number of friends. I think he liked that, as it made me more dependent on him.

I started having some sort of life so he would be jealous. He would have to put me down in order to stop me from fully embracing my newfound friendship groups. They were all on Facebook at the time, in the early days when Friends Reunited had been phased out. But I wouldn't dare go on it. He didn't want me to. A way of isolating me. It would allow me to see what was going on in the outside world. It would make me realise that there was more to life than being just a mum and a lover. To look good when he wanted to parade me to his friends. Then be able to put me back in my box for the rest of the time. He didn't want me to realise It was ok for me to be my own person and have my own interests.

The constant comparison to other women was draining. They were often only slightly prettier or thinner than I was. But it was enough for me to feel devalued. He wanted a Stepford wife. Someone who will do more than him in the home but always look good. Give good sex whenever he wants. I had to provide everything a woman should provide. Put up with his family drama. Smile sweetly.

He would put me down in front of others and make me feel small. He was a nightmare quite honestly. I had no hope of ever matching up to be the perfect wifey material. Who would be? He was quite open about it too. When friends would quiz him about his selfishness, he would own it, because he was the 'alpha.' He knew best and that was that.

He was almost proud of himself for the way he was. He always said that he was never dumped, he was the dumper with women, almost to be taken as a threat.

Eventually, the 'King of the Castle' act started to fall on the kids. He would always want the kids to prefer him over me. To the point where he would ask the kids to say whether he was liked more than their mum. He wasn't joking either. I remember when my son was only 4 or 5 years old, he would put him on the spot by asking him. You could see the fear in his poor little face, not knowing what to do. Do I say what my daddy wants to hear and upset mummy, or do I have daddy get cross? I hated what he was doing. What a way to make your kids feel. I would retaliate by telling him it wasn't appropriate and to stop, but he loved to make our son squirm and desperately needed to have another way to make me feel inferior, even as a mother.

Oddly enough, generally the one positive thing he would say about me at this point was that I was a wonderful mum. (Until we split up – then he painted me as the SHE devil but... that is something I will touch on soon)

His obsession started with what I ate. He would pick on my weight (I was a size 12). I became stressed about this and began going to the gym. I got down to size 8. Going to the gym four times a week to maintain it. He would still come up behind me and pinch the 'fat' I had on my waist, which was virtually zilch, but he loved to change the goal posts.

He later started to push this on my daughter. She wasn't allowed to have much and if she did eat it, she was scolded for eating so much. Once a brilliant eater, she started not eating as well. She would squirrel away some goodies and it became something she hid. I remember once, she was about 12 and she had gone to one of her friends for a sleepover. The next morning, he had gone through her bedroom doors and came downstairs with a handful of sweet wrappers. Acting like he was over the moon that he had caught her out. Something he could parade in front of the rest of the family to ridicule her with and make her feel small.

I tried my hardest to stick up for her. When you are the protective parent, it is so difficult to try and do when you have the other parent battling you at every turn. Co-parenting was impossible. It was more like counterparenting.

My son was a terrible eater. He ate nothing. Mealtimes became tedious. My partner would get annoyed and resort to giving him some chocolate buttons. No wonder his eating didn't improve over the years.

I decided enough was enough. I couldn't take it anymore. I told him that I didn't feel it was working and why (I had tried to tell him I was unhappy for a good year or so before it got to this point). He said he wouldn't do those things, but he just went back to his old ways each time. It was just lip service. He couldn't change, because this is who he was. I think it was the fact that his ego was truly dented that the real nastiness came out. Who am I to leave him? Who the hell do I think I am??

# CHAPTER 9
# REVENGE

He was not going to take this lying down. Instantly his true colours came out in full force. He told me I wouldn't be able to survive without him. If I go, then he will take my kids away from me. This is where he tried to keep me in this cycle. To trap me. That was the point of no return. He was blackmailing me to stay with him. He was blackmailing me. What the fuck!!!

Wow. This hit me with a ton of bricks...

I was devastated. He was making mine and my kids' lives a misery and here he was attacking the only self-worth I had left in that I was a good mum to my kids. I wanted to protect them. I hadn't been protected as a child, there was no way I wasn't going to try!

This resulted in a 10-year battle, a battle as the healthy parent, trying to protect our kids. The battle of having him continue to abuse. Locking me and the kids out of our home. The financial abuse by taking and fighting me in court. The constant hateful texts. The blackening of my name at my kids' schools. Going back to my past to speak to my ex-husband to gain some flying monkeys, getting him on side, making me look like a bad person throughout.

Pretending I was not my son's mother to the school authorities. These hateful letters in my son's school bag saying I was an unfit mother. The constant name-calling to my son about me.

Every birthday, holiday and visit was ruined by threats of not returning our son to me after visitation. The constant push for control long after we split up. I had dared to leave him and his 1950's lifestyle.

The withholding of my son's passport for the next 5 years. Another form of control, which meant I couldn't take our son and my daughter away to enjoy quality time as he had been able to with our son.

How he would try to move his current girlfriend into OUR house whilst destroying all of mine and my daughter's belongings.

He even invited my ex-husband and his wife to our house. Going through all my belongings like vultures, trying to pass off items of my clothing to his wife. I mean this is proper psycho behaviour. Something you would see in a film. Fatal attraction vibes. I can laugh at it now, but at the time I was in a state of shock that someone would stoop to these levels.

He was out of control and would do anything and everything he could to make my life hell, never once thinking about the effect all of this had on the children.

It didn't take long after we split up that my daughter had stopped seeing him of her own fruition. For a short while, she would visit when her brother went to see him and his family. She had thought of him like a father at one point, so she wanted it to remain the same, especially as she had already felt abandoned by her biological father. But when she visited, he would still go off on his golfing at the weekend, leaving them with his mother. Who dutifully did everything he asked.

Telephone calls between him and the children would consist of him badmouthing me. He did this with our 5-year-old also. Visits for my daughter became strained. They would consist of her stepnan following her around the house, in case she dared bring anything (that was hers) back home with her. She started treading on eggshells whilst she was there and, in the end, he pushed her away. He and his mother made her feel totally uncomfortable. He was trying to manipulate both kids to recruit them. But by doing it in a way that they were scared to do anything wrong by him. Sometimes under duress they would tell him what they wanted him to hear. This was devastating to me at times, but I knew what was happening and I felt helpless to help them. The systems in place to 'help' families get through this kind of stuff just enabled him to continue to abuse me and the children even more. They allowed him to manipulate and change the narrative to make me look like the bitter and twisted ex.

I was being put into a position where telling the truth of what was happening felt like it was a lie. He manipulated all the meetings with CAFCASS. (I would need another book to talk about that). Why could nobody see what was going on? Just as I thought I couldn't face any more sadness I would get another knife stuck inside me. I was hoping there would not be any more bad stuff thrown at me. But of course, this wasn't meant to be.

I had lost a shit load of weight. I was a shadow of my former self. I had to work nights to pay for my legal fees. I ate one meal a day. I would finish a 12-hour shift, get back to my parents, drive the kids to school which was 30 minutes away and then get back, go straight to sleep and get up again at half past 2 in the afternoon to do the school run again and in any spare time I had, I was putting together information for the court process I was going through. Life was brutal. It was harder than I could ever describe. It was taking its toll on me so much. I had gone down to weighing a mere 8 stone 9. My uniform for work was just hanging off me. I would be living on 5 hours of sleep a day and I *still* had to put a brave and happy face on for my kids. I couldn't let them see me so deflated and beaten. My solicitor's fees were astronomical and I hadn't had the best ordeal with them either. In fact, one of his solicitors, I knew. She was married to one of his friends. She said she would represent him, even though she had worked for me also. This was a breach on her part, as it was a conflict of interest.

My solicitors allowed this to go on for ages, even though this was the case. It was costing me many ££ requesting house paperwork that I knew they had. They were the original conveyancers you see. Yet they were not disclosing anything we were asking for. Dragging everything out as long as they possibly could.

To make things even more harrowing for me and the kids, my solicitor suddenly left halfway through the court hearings, so the more expensive one had to take over. More dents in my purse strings. Causing more and more stress on my mental health. It was relentless. They were going for the jugular at every step of the way. Like a Pitbull holding onto prey by its teeth. This felt like it was never going to stop. Will this never end? Will he get what he wants? If he doesn't get me one way, what else will he try to do? He had already got CAFCASS on his side. The mountain of evidence I had totally disregarded by them and the court.

They didn't even look at it.

He was awarded joint custody of our son. He couldn't be with my daughter as she was old enough by then to make her own decisions. I felt like my youngest was being thrown to the wolves, by the people who should be able to see past what was going on and do what is right for that child. Instead, he was dragged away from his sister. They allowed him to be used by his father all through his life.

Every birthday was ruined over the years. By antics to prevent him from coming home. Police had to be called a couple of times so I could get my son back. He would even send his girlfriend out (she was a copper ironically) to try and stall my son coming out for as long as possible on his birthday when he was in their care. I only had 2 hours, so by the time we had any chance of quality time, it was over. We were both left distressed by what his dad was doing.

I used to dread the holidays. Birthdays, Christmas. I think, even though a lot of time has passed now, I still feel dread when it comes to those types of holidays. The impact that time had on us all still lives with us in some form or another. You would have to be a robot to be able to just get over and move on from something like this. It wasn't like that was all I had to deal with, I still had to deal with unresolved trauma from my childhood too. How I managed to get through any of that is still unknown. There were a few times when I felt I couldn't. I will be honest with you, there were times when I felt maybe my kids would be better off without me.

Maybe I was the one who had made all this happen (childhood trauma coming out). If I wasn't here, then ok, they would be with him, but it might be better because he wouldn't be spending his days fighting me. I would try to go to sleep between shifts. It would take me a good while before I could nod off. I would often picture myself in my car, driving full pelt into a tree. To block out all the pain I was enduring. I was tired. I was not being heard by the authorities. I was getting into serious debt. I wasn't eating well, I was exhausted. I was crying out for help, but no one would

Yet, I carried on. I endured more abuse and the more it went on the more I was faltering. I was fading away. I just couldn't see an end to it.

I felt like I had been hit by a brick. The best way I can describe it is my head felt like it was being held in a vice and someone was there, squeezing it in second by second. I am surprised I hadn't combusted. The pressure I felt was something I had never experienced before. The childhood trauma I had never dealt with. Things were done to me, but I didn't put up a fight. I didn't know how to, or that I should.

No one was hearing me or considering the seriousness of it. How was this happening? How can this be the way it is? Silenced in speaking my truth again. It didn't benefit anyone to have the truth told, because it didn't serve THEM well for me to be heard. Solicitors because of all the money they were raking in, the courts because men rule in this kind of world and women are simply neurotic. He was given joint custody and therefore continued to make our lives hell. We had been fighting as long as we had been together. How is that for perspective?

That has got to be nuts in anyone's book.

The disaster of a breakup. Court battles, shit load of money spent, just to get what I was rightfully owed. This was the worst I could ever feel. Or so I thought.

# CHAPTER 10
# END OF THE ROAD

I could never understand how someone who once claimed to love me could be so callous to want to see us destitute and homeless.

I had never attempted suicide but as I had mentioned, I had imagined it many times.

The main reason I didn't was my children. How could I leave them to have all that grief put on them knowing that neither child would have the support to get them through it. I don't think I actually wanted to go through with it, I just felt that the pain was too much to bear and I didn't know how I would be able to come back from all this hurt. I felt like a failure. Here I was again, trusting the wrong person. Why was I so stupid to fall for someone who was not good for me. The trouble was, I listened to words. I wanted so much to be loved and looked after that I would accept breadcrumbs. I felt that this was all I was worth. Let's face it. No-one saved me from my childhood abuse, but I kept hoping someone would eventually come and save me at some point. Surely, I can't keep attracting people with hidden agendas. Surely someone would truly love me without there being a price on my head? But each time I tried, I was always met with control, hate and spite.

Another 5 years went by after separating. I finally got a home for myself and my kids in September 2014. Mortgage free because at last someone had ruled in my favour.

2017 I decided to meet someone again. I had felt I was ready to start dating.

My daughter had left home by then to live with her boyfriend. I had every other weekend to do things for myself. Most of my friends were in couples, so I was the only single out of my circle.

I met someone on a dating website. This was alien to me. I never wanted to find someone that way, but by that time, everything was online. You rarely meet anyone the conventional way anymore. I had been on a few dates. I started chatting to this man. He was a little older than me (7 years) and he came across as very articulate. He appeared to have a good job. Had his shit together. Was in his own place, he could pay his own bills and just seemed like a well-balanced person.

We chatted for a while before we arranged to meet. But we ended up meeting one Sunday morning at a coffee shop. I had been out with the girls the night before so wasn't shall we say, feeling at my best, but instead of cancelling, as I hated letting anyone down (people pleasing) we both rocked up and I felt instantly attracted to him. I had belly flutters, so I was happy that I had turned up. He gave me a kiss on the cheek, and we walked into the coffee shop. He was tall and slim, which I liked, and something I noticed about him was that he had a soft voice, so I associated that with him being kind and gentle. Boy did I wish I had cancelled this date, if I had known, if only I had known. But I didn't. These people can smell vulnerability from a mile off. Like prey, seeking out those they can dominate. Every man I had been in a relationship with. ALL had childhood issues in some way. This came out in adulthood of always needing to control everything and everyone to stop themselves feeling less than. They treated others like shit and didn't care about the disaster they left behind. If they were winning, morals went out of the window. You see abusive people MUST have control over everything and whenever they did have a conscience about what they were doing, it would be short-lived because it was seen by them as a weakness. So, they would continue to be destructive and this became part of normal behaviour.

Little did I know what was to come...

So, when we had finished the date, I remembered him giving me a kiss, only a peck and I thought I had met someone really nice.

We chatted for a bit and then he disappeared for a while. Possibly around 3 weeks to a month or something like that. I was ready to give up and sent my last message; if he doesn't reply, I will move on. I wished more than anything that I had sent it.

So after being on my own for all this time. I thought I had healed. I realise now that I was nowhere near healed. I hadn't dealt with anything. I guess being brought up by people who didn't deal with anything, I brushed everything under the carpet, that is exactly what I had done. I brushed myself off, put a fake smile on my face and carried on. Same as I did as a kid. Oblivious to all the hurt I was feeling, because that is what I was used to. I locked it away, never to be returned to again. That I guess, was the only way I could deal with each day. If I constantly dwelled on the horrid past, I wouldn't be able to function. I lived my life in functional freeze and in survival mode. I just didn't realise it.

After a few weeks or so we continued chatting and eventually he asked me if I wanted to meet him. I said yes. As it got nearer to the date, he dropped in that his mum and stepdad would be there. I was totally taken aback by this, as I thought that was a bit much, given we knew little of each other, but I still went. Again, not perceiving any possibility of danger. He said I could stay there and I guess I naively thought as his parents were there, he must be ok and I guess I felt safe in the fact they were there. When I look back, I don't even know what I was thinking, I was so desperate to feel genuine connection and love, that again, I listened to the words, not picking up on the red flags that now I know were so apparent. They were illuminating him, but I didn't see them. I feel so sad for that little girl who just wanted to feel loved, that I believed in the fairytale that was surrounding me as a child through Disney and other unrealistic films/programmes about how love should be and how, surely by now, this was it, finally I would find my person and be happy. That is all I ever wanted. Just to be happy. Surely that is not too much to ask? Surely God wouldn't put me through any more shit? Surely, I'd had enough and now was my time?

I got to his house, he had a nice house, met his parents, shared wine with them and they appeared respectable, it looked like they all got on well, so I thought they had a close relationship, or at least that is how he was portraying it. Little did I know that it couldn't be further from the truth. Yes, they performed in front of others as a close-knit family. But deep down they were far from that but obviously I didn't find that out until much later.

Time went on and he often went on biking holidays with other fellow bikers. We had been going out for about 3 months and I thought we were doing well. He said all the right things, he said he loved me and when he was away, he was attentive, he called me every day or so. He would ask me how I was and genuinely I thought we were happy.

He later became quite intense. He would be great most of the time, but then every so often, he would show a bit of anger. An ex of mine had asked to meet up with me. We only knew each other for a short time, but he contacted me out of the blue, as he wanted to speak to me, to explain why he had ghosted me at the time we dated. ( I had a few dates with him before this relationship, so it was short-lived as he had a mountain of problems) and I felt sorry for him and also needed to soothe *my* need of being helpful.

I would try to fix him, so I said I would meet him, to hear him out. I knew I wasn't interested in getting back with him as he had disappeared without a trace, so I didn't feel I wanted to give him another chance or anything, so I met him and he said his piece - I said mine. He was full of regret, but that was that. No more contact.

Time passed and the new boyfriend had been drinking copious amounts of wine. He had been on my phone, and accusations of infidelity were becoming more regular, but usually alcohol induced, so again another huge red flag that I ignored. I kid myself that it was just alcohol and he isn't normally like that, so it must be that. He had seen on my phone that I had liked someone's post and went ballistic, we argued and then he threw my phone across the living room and my screen broke into little pieces, I couldn't switch my phone on. I needed my phone, like most people do. My whole life was on it. He apologised profusely and the next day, I went back home to my house and had to sort out the damage. It cost me over £200 to get a new one, which I couldn't really afford, but what more could I do, I needed to have it.

Whilst I was trying to sort it out with EE, he was phoning me. I could feel panic because I had missed his call. Already, I was treading on eggshells, my heart was beating out of my chest and my hands were shaking. I was a mess. He accused me of doing something I shouldn't be and I found myself arguing the toss with him, trying to plead my case of honesty. It was like I was on trial. I was accused of so much shit and made to feel it was my fault. I had a past, and the past was always used against me. I couldn't win. I can't tell you the emotional roller-coaster I was on but didn't realise at this stage it was abuse. Because he wasn't always like this. A lot of the time he would be kind and gentle and it was those parts of him that I clung onto. He wasn't a monster, he was just someone who had a short fuse... He would say it was because he loved me *too* much.

The red flags came thick and fast, but I still hadn't realised. I started to believe it was me who had the problem and I constantly had to defend myself about who I was and how good a person I was because I was being called all sorts.

You see all the shouting and arguments I endured were out of the norm for me. Although I had shitty controlling relationships in the past, they had never really been argumentative ones and I didn't know how to deal with them, so I would try to pacify him, own 'I did wrong' just to stop all the animosity that was building. After calling me all sorts of horrid names, I would cry and run to a bedroom to get away from him and he would leave me there upset, but then after a while, he would come up to see me and suddenly be all lovely again. His way of making it up to me was having sex with me. He wouldn't listen to me and how upset I was, he would just have sex and then forget and expect me to forget so we could move on from it. This became a regular occurrence. If I wasn't with him, he would flare up accusing me of having affairs with someone else.

He would want video proof that I was at home and on my own. It was totally fucking crazy, but the emotional highs and lows kept me trapped. I spent more time defending myself than any relationship I had been in before. Slowly but surely, he would come up with things that I hadn't told him. He just knew things. I had no clue how. I remember being at his for a weekend and he tricked me into going onto Facebook and logging in to my account, I can't quite remember how he got me to do it, but by this time, I was so weary of setting him off with anger outbursts, that I pretty much did what he said. As I had added my info in, I was on it for a bit and then he asked to have it back (the iPad was his). I didn't think anything of it and just carried on watching TV in bed.

Time went on and I would stay with him quite regularly. I would fall asleep at night and he would always, without fail, go on his iPad before bed. What I didn't realise was he was stalking my Facebook account, trying to 'dig out dirt' on me to use at a later date. Many times, I would fall asleep only to wake up at 3 in the morning with the light still on and he was still on the iPad. I would ask him, why are you not asleep? He would look at me with his dark piercing eyes and tell me how I was cheating on him and how I had done something wrong. There he would be, in the middle of the night, calling me a cunt, putting the fear of God in me. I would be crying, protesting my innocence yet again. This would go on for hours, accusations flying from every direction. Me yet again defending myself, exhausted, trying to plead with him that I was a good person and that I wasn't the horrible things he said I was. Eventually he would stop and we would fall asleep. I would often cry myself to sleep and for a while, he would then want to make up, again by having sex with me. He would do things that I wasn't happy with, but I dared not say anything because I was in fear that it would start all over again. I had to respond in the way he wanted me to, to avoid further confrontation. He terrified me yet I was totally trauma bonded to him. I was under his spell, from fear. I was powerless to walk away, oh how I wish I had walked away.

Why did I stay? I just didn't know why I would put up with such disgusting behaviour, but I did. The cycle would repeat. The constant eggshells and fear. Survival was my only form of defence. I couldn't walk away; it was almost like I didn't have an option. The fear and survival mode were just keeping me safe in that moment. I didn't know what else to do.

I didn't tell anyone about what was happening, because I was ashamed that I was in another coercive relationship and could not see a way out. I was being controlled. I somehow felt I couldn't cope on my own anymore and the guilt for my kids and the shame that I couldn't have a decent loving relationship. I thought this was all I was good for. My self-worth was at an all-time low. I was a bag of nerves, and I couldn't say anything to anyone. What was I going to do? I was at a total loss. The little girl inside of me was yet again wanting to be saved from all this fear and heartache, but no one stepped forward. I became a shell on the inside. I felt trapped. I felt I was letting my children down. I felt like a total failure. Why did I feel so tied to this man? Why can I not leave him? I didn't have the answers. I was in constant fight or flight mode. My heart would race. I was on alert, waiting for the next signs of danger.

# CHAPTER 11
# THE STORM

As time went on, the abuse heightened. He would go weeks giving me the silent treatment. He would contact me if we were not together to tell me I was having affairs behind his back. I was in fear of speaking to anyone, male OR female in the end. Every time my mobile phone rang, he would question me as to who it was. Even now after 5 years, I still have moments where my heart races when my phone rings or a text comes through. The lasting effects abuse has on you are hard for anyone to truly understand who hasn't been through it.

He would stalk my every move, I felt he had eyes on me everywhere. How can one individual instil so much fear and still base it around love? Make you think, it is only because he cares about you so much that it makes him do the things he does.

He once said to me that he has a lot of demons that he is dealing with. A moment where I thought he was opening up, where I thought I could understand him better. I tried to show him compassion, even though he was someone who had zero compassion for me and the things he was putting me through. Of course, any moments of vulnerability from him, he would later deny. Gaslighting me, telling me I was making it all up and that it didn't happen. Telling me I am stupid and how thick I am. Belittling me at every opportunity.

Eventually, he pushed me into moving in with him. I gave up everything for him, out of total fear and he did his utmost to remove every part of independence I had. He was in my bank accounts, he was in my emails, he had access to my phone and any other device I had. Accessing them without my control. I had no option but to continue being monitored. So many people across society say, "Why don't you just leave?" but it doesn't work like that. They do it in such an insidious way that you don't realise that they were grooming you from the start. They exert power and control over you without you even realising it, until one day you are on your own. You have been isolated; you have been conditioned to understand that you are locked in. No one will believe you, because on the outside, he came across as a decent, gentle, helpful human being, but behind closed doors, he was a monster.

Towards the end of our relationship, he vamped up his exert of power. He had such a manipulative way of turning everything around to be my fault. I was the problem, not him. He would further use sex to control me. I had no idea that what he was doing was rape. He would yell at me for hours, call me terrible names, keep me awake all night, turning lights on, playing music until the early hours, so loudly that the whole house would shake. All to keep me in a fear state, sleep deprived, then insist I had sex with him. If I didn't he would prolong 'the argument', he would act like he was holding out an olive branch and I was the one who was continuing the animosity by saying no. I was forced into having sex with him, or I would have to suffer the consequences. I was not in any way giving consent. I would be coerced into having sex with him to prevent being punished further. He told me that if I left him, his solicitors would 'annihilate me.' The sad thing was he wasn't wrong about that. He kept his word through all of it.

One night, he had shouted at me for 6 hours straight, he had gone through the silent treatment for a good couple of weeks beforehand and I had waited for him to go to sleep and then I went to bed, trying to slip into the covers so lightly so as not to wake him up. It was literally like a ticking time bomb. One false move and I could blow myself up....

This would be one of those nights.

He decided he was going to let rip at me again. He hurled abuse at me, he was like a caged animal. He called me a cunt, more times than I could ever tell you. As I said before, he would every night be going through my social media, trying to find ammunition to hit me with, to prove that I wasn't a loyal girlfriend. It flared up and he made me cry uncontrollably by his disgusting words and sleep deprivation. He would turn the light on (I couldn't sleep in a light room and would have to have blackout blinds) so having the light on meant that I would be wide awake. I would ask him to turn it off, but I would get a barrage of insults thrown at me. Lack of sleep and constant nasty threats made my head feel like it was going to explode. I was worn down, I felt defeated, I felt crushed. I had nothing left in me to continue this way. I was exhausted. I would be in floods of tears and he would be so callous and nasty. He got off on this, it just made him continue more and more and act more and more vicious. Eventually I just couldn't take it anymore, it was like torture, I got up and tried to turn his side lamp off myself. I went to the switch at the side of his bed and he literally grabbed my hand so tight, it was hurting and he would not let go. He was so much stronger than I was, and he grabbed onto my hand for dear life and refused to have that light off. I was trying to pull away, but he continued to fight with me, keeping my hand attached to his, so much so that eventually the wire for the light snapped in half. Not pulled out from the root of the socket, but literally from halfway. I was in total shock. I ran into the spare bedroom and just cried. I sobbed; my face was all swollen from sobbing so hard. I felt like I must have cried for hours and eventually I cried myself to sleep. He, of course, slept like a baby instantly and revelled in the fact that he had broken me. He enjoyed it. He showed no remorse the next day. He would do all of that and then the next day act as though he hadn't done anything. He got up for work like normal the next day, like nothing had happened.

By this point I was a nervous wreck. I still had to go to work and try to act normally, but it was getting harder and harder. I was a broken person.

I would be the one to do the meals in the evening and it was a bit of a game for him to not let me know when he was coming home from work, it was to keep me on my toes, to keep me treading on eggshells. Never knowing what mood he would be in. As soon as I heard his vehicle come around the corner, my heart would jump again. This was a regular thing, I had traits of PTSD, just from the sound of his engine.

He would come in from work and I would anxiously go to the kitchen (as he would always go in through the back gate). He would purposely take his time. He had a routine, he wanted to take as long as possible before he acknowledged me, he would slowly take his helmet off, check both his phones. He always had 2 (or more) and he would meticulously check them, all without saying a word. He would then bypass me and go into the toilet and I would be standing there like a lemon, waiting for a little crumb of decency from him to acknowledge that I was there to greet him. Often, still ignoring me, he would go over to the dinner I was cooking and then look at it with disgust and tell me that he had already eaten that at lunchtime, at work. I would say I didn't know that as he hadn't told me and he would push the plate across the worktop with the glare of hate. Eggshells felt more like broken glass. He couldn't make me feel any more shit than I did at that moment.

He would chip away at me constantly. In subtle and not-so-subtle ways. There was another incident where he didn't talk to me for weeks. I would cook him dinner, I would be in the living room and he would leave my dinner on the side and go and make himself a different meal and walk up to the bedroom, all without saying a word. As I say, this went on for 3 weeks and then one morning, I think it was either Mother's Day or it was his mum's birthday. Whatever it was, unbeknown to me, he (we) was supposed to be going to visit his mum. His brothers were going too and he expected me to go with him and play happy families, so that his image to his family could be upheld. I was in such a bad state from all the incidents before, so there was no way I could go and pretend that everything was ok. It won't be alright. It was far from being alright. I said no and of course he flew off the handle again and told me angrily that I was a selfish cunt. The look of total contempt and disgust and with that just left.

After a few days, he had decided that he now wanted to play Mr. Nice, to throw another imbalance of power. Out of fear, I had to go along with it, or I would reap the punishment again. I had to pacify him as much as I could to not have to go through yet another showdown. He was totally in control of everything and my job here was to be on guard to find my way through another vicious episode from him, but of course, the calm was short lived, as the next episode was on its way.

It was only about a week after the previous episode that the next one was brewing. This was in March 2019. I had bought him some local comedy night tickets for Valentine's Day (which was ruined on the day) and having only just gone through another incident with silent treatment, he said he still wanted to go to this event. We did and so far, it went ok, he decided that he wanted to go into town and continue the evening at a bar. Whilst we were in there, he started talking about wanting to marry me, a complete contrast to his behaviour over the months and I was yet again confused. He kept repeating he wanted to marry me and I was in complete confusion, as he had been treating me like total shit for so long. Why is he now saying all of this? Stupidly I said to him, thinking he was giving me an olive branch, that if he truly wanted to marry me, then the cruel outbursts needed to stop, as I can't marry someone who does those things to me. He then snapped back, telling me that again *I* was ruining what we had. Here I am again, pushing him away when he was being nice to me... The fear of dread set in again, fight or flight mode again had kicked in. We moved over to a corner of the bar, on some barstools and he would not talk to me. In these split seconds, my brain is going ten to a dozen, wondering how the hell I was going to handle this as I knew it was all going to end badly. When he went out that night, he told me not to bring any purse out and he had my house keys in his pocket the whole evening. He got up and went to the toilet, so I started to panic and wanted to grab my keys in case he was going to do something nasty. Within seconds he was back and of course caught me trying to get my keys back. He gave me the dirtiest look, grabbed his jacket back and walked out of the bar, leaving me in there on my own. I was panicking, what the hell was I going to do now. I have no money, I have no keys to get into my house. I had no choice but to leave the bar too. I couldn't stay in a bar at 1am in the morning, I had no choice but to go home.

I came out of the bar and it was absolutely pissing down with rain. I could see his silhouette from a distance, he did not look back, he just continued to walk to our house, not giving a shit as to where I was or if I was walking home alone. Eventually he came out of sight and I remember walking up to the road where our property was and all sorts of things were going on in my mind. Can I get in, has he locked me out? If I do get in, what do I do when I get there, what will HE do when I get in there? I was so scared and hypervigilant as to what I might be met with. I tried the door and to my amazement, the door was unlocked, I slowly walked in and I realised he was in the toilet which was located just to the right of the hallway by the front door.

I decided to just go straight up to my son's room as he was away this weekend. I got into bed, heart racing. I heard him come out of the toilet and go into the living room. He had picked up some more alcohol from the fridge beforehand and he then put music on. He turned it up so loudly, the house shook again. He did this many times throughout our relationship to make sure I could not sleep. But I thought, maybe he will stay down there for a while and sleep off the drink... I put my head under the covers and decided to look for the number of the Domestic abuse helpline. I bottled it by phoning them, because I was worried he would know, as he was clearly on my phone on a regular basis. I tried ringing one of my friends as I had confided in her a week or two before that this was happening. She had told me to phone her any time if anything kicked off, but she didn't answer. I left her a message, put my phone on silent. Within a few minutes the music stopped and I heard him coming upstairs. I had to think quickly, so I put my phone in my son's underwear drawer as I knew if the phone went, I would have no chance of getting out of this unscathed. He burst in and pushed the door so hard that the handle cracked the wall.

He was shouting and screaming at me, telling me what a horrible cunt I was and demanding to have my phone, he was saying to me that my cousin had messaged me saying something which had meant I was doing something untoward, I knew this isn't the case, as my cousin and I were not close enough for me to tell her what was happening in my life and I refused to tell him where the phone had gone. I got up off the bed and tried to move away from him but he had cornered me by the window in the bedroom. He was fuming and in such a rage. His eyes were dark and screwed up, the look of hatred in his face. He had me there and he lifted his arm up (he was 6ft and I am 5 '5, so considerably taller than I am) and he had pulled his arm up as though he was going to punch me in my face. I screamed at him to stop but he continued to glare at me holding his fist clenched up by his ear ready to throw me a punch. I didn't know what to do, so I just screamed " Bloody do it then. If you're going to punch me, just do it and get it over with."

He shoved me on the floor with his other hand and my legs just buckled. I fell back and tried to stop myself from falling by putting my hand down to take the fall and I was on the ground. I yelled that he had hurt my hand, the pain was shooting through my palm and up my arm and I knew he had hurt me. He ignored it and said nothing. He had moved away slightly so I ran towards the bedroom door, flew downstairs to get out of the house, for fear of what was to happen next. He somehow managed to get in front of me on the stairs and at this time we were down the bottom. There were about 3 steps left before the staircase ended. I was in fear for my life. He had put me in a position where I could not get away. He was leaning over me, we had no carpet on the stairs at this time, as the house was new and we hadn't got around to finishing it yet. He had his face right in front of my own, he had his legs either side of mine and his arms either side of my arms, I was locked in position. I had my hands over my face, scared for my life. I was screaming, please don't hurt me, please don't hurt me and I truly thought this was it. He was going to kill me, my life literally flashed before my eyes.

Then suddenly it went quiet. It was eerily quiet.

I took my hands away from my face slowly as he got off me. He sat at the bottom of the stairs, back to the wall of the staircase and his legs were laid out in front of him blocking the bottom of the stairs. I couldn't move from fear, he was literally just sitting there in silence, staring into space. I tried to ask him why he would do that to me, trying to reason with a psychopath, clearly isn't something you can do, but I wanted to try to make him see what he was doing, but he said nothing. It felt like we were sitting there for ages, I was in disbelief about what had just happened. Eventually, he just got up, walked past me on the stairs, got to the top of the stairs and just simply said, "Meet me halfway, come to bed." I just froze, what the hell was I supposed to do? I'd had a couple of drinks at the beginning of the night, so although I hadn't had much, I couldn't drive anywhere. What was I supposed to do? I was shaking. Not knowing how I needed to protect myself, I walked upstairs to the bed he was in. He instantly went to sleep... I mean wtf. How does someone do all of that and go straight to sleep? I got into bed as slowly as I possibly could, my whole hand and arm was throbbing so badly, I wasn't sure if it was broken, or not. I literally laid there, fully dressed, scared to move all night. I lay there wide awake, whilst he slept like a baby. It got to about 7.30am and I decided to slip out of bed. I needed to get away from him, I needed to be safe. I went downstairs and found my keys were still in his jacket pocket which he had laid on the bannister the night before, I literally had the key in the back door, to leave and go to my car which I had parked up near the high street the night before, not knowing what my next move was going to be, then he suddenly appeared behind me. "Where are you going?'" he asked. I said I needed to remove myself and have time to think. He got angry again and said if I walked out the door now, he would not allow me back in. I grabbed the keys out of the door and ran out of the house and made my way along the main road, checking behind me in case he was following me. My heart was pounding, in fact, I don't think it had ever stopped from the previous night, but I carried on walking. I phoned my friend again but this time it was about 8am. Surely, she would be up and answer the phone, but she didn't. I didn't know what to do as I hadn't told anyone else, but I tried another friend.

I was just sitting in my car, I had moved it so it couldn't be seen at the side of the main road. She didn't answer either, but she did phone me back a few minutes later. She was shocked. As I was talking to her, the phone rang and it was him. My heart sank, I didn't know what to do. I was scared to answer it. Then I got a text. It literally just said, "What do you want for breakfast, salmon and eggs??", I mean what the actual fuck was I to do with that. I sat there for a while trying to gather my thoughts.

I ended up going back, as I didn't know what to do. It was my home, I had already had one ex lock me out never for me to enter again, keeping my belongings etc. If I didn't go back, I would likely have the same issues again. When I arrived there, he was calm, acting like nothing had happened. He came up to me and said he loved me and he wouldn't do that again. He said he would get help and he realised he had a problem. By this time, I didn't believe a word of it, but I had to play along as I had no choice but to survive the best I could until I could get some advice on what I needed to do next.

He stood in front of me, rubbing my hair in a really eerie way. Almost like he was stroking a cat like in one of those Bond films. One hand after another, smoothing my hair down, almost like he was slicking it back with gel or something. It was the most surreal thing.

I could do nothing but bide my time as to what I could do to keep myself as safe as I possibly could. I decided to speak to the DA helpline one day when he was at work. This took a lot of courage and it had taken me all week to give them a call, to ask them some advice and to see if they felt what I had experienced was DV. I was still unsure.

They confirmed that it was and I needed to go to the police when it was safe to do so. It was a Friday and he had his daughters coming over for food on the weekend along with his grandkids. I thought, I will just get this weekend over and then I will go to the police. Just get through this last time.....

Saturday arrived and his kids turned up, smiles all round, playing the part of the good, dutiful girlfriend I was meant to be. My hand was throbbing. His Granddaughter who was about 1 at the time, kept coming up to me, wanting me to hold her and I tried so hard to hide the fact that I was in pain. I would nurse my hand on my lap and try to lift her with one arm, in the hope no one would notice.

He had 2 daughters and a son. One was almost like me. The black sheep, the outsider. They always said she had funny ways, but maybe she was the only one who wouldn't conform to the family bullshit. It was her that I felt most close to. I always felt the other kept me at arm's length. Looking back, maybe it was because she knew history would repeat itself. Eventually either I would be discarded, or I would be forced out of the relationship because of her violent father. Either way, I was aware of the difference.

I should have got an Oscar award for that day with his kids. No one would know how anxious I was feeling, how I knew that I would be reporting him to the Police on Monday. Finally, doing what I needed to do to keep me safe. Looking back now, I think he had an inkling something was going to happen. I don't think he knew what, but he could feel it in the energy, I am pretty sure of that.

It is funny, but not uncommon just how many families turn a blind eye. ALL of them would know what he was, what he was capable of, but every one of them kept quiet. Friends of his ALL knew what he was, but did the same.

For a long time, I felt quite hurt by this. I certainly felt let down by it. One of his friends turned up at our house after we split up. The look on his friend's face when he realised. His face literally went grey, because he knew, yet said nothing. They all knew and said nothing. Those people, the abusers flying monkeys, all did their role perfectly. They played an absolute blinder, all of them.

I would go through a mixture of emotions over the months when I would think about it all. Although most of the time, I would rather not think about it, as it would highlight how much I was alone, yet again. Being alone in my time of need. To defend myself alone. How much I had been let down by so many and how angry I was that everyone treated me like shit, like I was nothing. All whilst pretending to be the opposite.

The time came and his family left. Now what do I do? I had to try and keep the peace, hoping that I could stretch it out until Monday when he went to work. Of course this did not happen. They left and he decided to get the drink out some more. He kept pouring me drinks, he kept filling up his. I didn't want to drink particularly as I wanted my wits about me but was scared that if I looked like I wasn't drinking then he would be suspicious.

He was in no way ready to stop, so I drank some more but eventually decided I couldn't drink anymore and I went to bed, whilst he continued, sinking the red wine. Stupidly without realising, I left my phone down the stairs where he was sitting. Going back down wasn't an option.

As I fell asleep, I was suddenly woken up, he was shouting at me again, "You fucking cunt, you fucking cunt, I have just seen a message. I knew you were cheating; I knew you were."

Now I knew he was again making shit up, just so he had a reason to lay into me. I jumped out of bed asking what on earth he was talking about and he kept repeating this message I had received on my phone.

So, I challenged him to show me what was on my phone and what was in my message. We sat on the sofa and there he was scrolling through my phone like a maniac, wanting to find something he could confront me with so it would excuse his violent and aggressive behaviour. Of course, there was nothing. Yet again I am awoken by his outbursts. Him trying to find some shit on me to warrant his further abuse. To demoralise me, to belittle me, to accuse me. To wear me down. A repeated pattern that just kept coming back. Luckily I somehow managed to pacify him enough to calm him down and he got into bed.

Next day, I tried to act like nothing had happened. Trying to get through every second as best I could. One more day I thought, one more day and then hopefully this would be over.... It wasn't. Reporting it was just the beginning.

There was a Police Investigation that took months. The lack of contact, one minute I'm a high-risk case, the next medium to low. Paladin, a service helping victims of stalking, would tell me how much danger I was in, but for the Police to take the necessary steps, well, that was nearly impossible. The promises of what they were going to do, the death threats received, the stalking, the fear I was feeling, the isolation. The lack of contact with the police. The feeling they don't take me or the situation seriously enough. Always feeling like everyone thinks I am neurotic and misguided. It felt at times that I was seen as the criminal and not the perpetrator. Being continually let down by the system.

He was arrested twice over the months. On both occasions the results ended up as an NFA (No further action), due to lack of enough evidence. He got away with it. He is free to continue his abuse of me, but also to continue to avenge his next victim. I dread to think how many times he has mistreated another human being (female of course, because above everything he is a weak man and the only way he can feel like a man is to demean and violate a woman). The justice system has allowed another to walk free. Given a free pass to humiliate and violate another and not only that, be rewarded for it. This will then bring me on to the next stage of my story.

# CHAPTER 12
# JUST THE BEGINNING

Court start dates were limited due to COVID hitting. This added to the torment of the abuse he was still managing to inflict upon me. He had a solicitor who had a threatening nature to them. Critical of me and doing cheap shots at me via solicitors' letters. The number of times my solicitor would say, "Now don't worry about what they are saying, this is what we need to do etc." I was exhausted. How can I be put through this type of abuse all over again? Haven't I suffered enough? I used to think. The number of times I was degraded and ridiculed, not only in fear of the abuser turning up at my home, but I also had the threats from his solicitors, adding on more and more pressure.

My brain was full, I was getting to breaking point. How I survived this I do not know, but I had to. I had to find a way.

The time it took to even get to court. He played dirty at every step and as expected, the courts just allowed him to. This enabled him, just like all his friends and family did, except this time, the decisions were going to be up to them. My life is literally in the family court's hands.

I remember going into court, my daughter came with me and she sat in the waiting room throughout. It was a two-day court hearing, just to prolong the shit show longer. It was drawn out so much.

He turned up with his brother. I could hear him whilst I was in the waiting room waiting to be called in. Talking about me, saying to his brother what a cunt I was. No matter how many times I hear that word being said about me, each time it is like he is driving a knife into my heart, chipping away at me continuously, hoping that I would break into a million pieces...

Many times, I felt like giving up. On the court case, on my home, on my life... but I had to keep going. I had to...

I was on the stand; I was allowed to have a screen as I don't think I could've coped seeing his dark evil eyes staring at me whilst I talked about the unthinkable. His barrister was an old man and to be quite honest with you, considering he was doing the job he does; he didn't appear to really know what he was doing. Nevertheless, he continually quizzed me on the witness stand for most of the day. Presumably trying to weigh me down. Just like the abuser has... you know, push her a little more, then some more and then a bit more, just to watch me crack.

Considering what we were there for, and the fact the abuser and his solicitors were able to request more information when we had already submitted the information requested and the deadline had to be met (or so I thought), it turns out that wasn't the case. I had played by the rules of the court. He didn't. Yet he was allowed to request more. I literally got the request at 8pm the night before the court hearing and a HUGE bundle I had to try and trawl through. As you can probably imagine, having waited so long and the emotional rollercoaster I was going through, this was just adding to it, which clearly was its intent. To create more fear ahead of the court day.

Family court is an absolute mess, but I would be here all day telling you about the issues surrounding family court and the misogyny and foul play that fuels this type of court hearing. I would need to write another book on that one :)

Day 1 and the interrogation started. Given what we were there about, the spotlight was on me and the fact he raped me. This was his solicitor's continual line of questioning to me. Constantly telling me what a liar I was, how I wasn't raped. How *I* was using him to gain financially, even though it was me who had everything to lose. It was going to be MY life that would be in tatters, he stood everything to gain, with me OR without me. All my money was tied up in our house. He lied through his teeth like a true psychopath. The lies literally rolled off his tongue. He lied about the house, the amount of the financials, how I was the abuser, all the things that I know now are textbook behaviours, but the court lapped up the whole lot and I paid the price deeply, in more ways than one. But still he acted like he was an angel and they lapped it up. Every single word, without evidence to back it up, they just took his word. The word vomit coming out of his mouth you would think Mother Teresa was standing up there the way they just took it all in without question. Don't get me wrong, my solicitor gave it his all when it came to cross-examining him the next day, but he just spoke utter crap and the judge allowed him to get away with it even when it was obvious he was lying. I thought lying was contempt of court legally, but in family court, this doesn't seem to be taken into consideration. Sadly, this behaviour is all too common, especially when there is abuse and rape involved. The victim is guilty until proven innocent, yet the perpetrator is innocent despite all the evidence to the contrary.

After it was all over, I was escorted to the ladies by my Barrister as I really needed to use the toilet, he walked with me and stood outside whilst I was in there. When I came out, he told me something bizarre. The perpetrator's brother shook his hand and congratulated him on his sterling work. I mean what the actual fuck!!!! Who does that? Honestly, the behaviour of everyone was unbelievable.

Even worse, the judge decided to make a decision **after** the court case and I had the gruelling wait for a whole fucking month to hear the verdict. A whole fucking month... How disgusting is that? Prolonging the agony, yet again.

The verdict came in and I just wept. I sobbed and I sobbed. He had done it. He had got what he wanted. He had been given permission to screw me over one last time. He was awarded everything. My whole life was ripped apart from me and my children. I had no money, I had debt up to my eyeballs and I was now homeless. What the fuck was I going to do now. I had to pay HIS solicitors fees. His lies meant that I had to give him more money for other losses that they were unable to prove. Devastation was not even coming close. I was at an all-time low. My life was in tatters and I had nothing left to give.

The worst had happened. The courts had managed to rip me apart into a billion pieces. My body ached but was numb at the same time. How was I going to cope? How was I going to get through this hell hole called life? How was I going to face this world anymore? I always felt alone but then I felt despair like never before. How could this possibly have been allowed to happen?

Day-to-day living was excruciating. I felt shame, I felt guilt, I felt like such a stupid person. I was abused and I felt like a bad person!?!

**NO** victim of abuse should ever be made to feel like they deserved it, that they asked for it nor feel that only bad people get on in life and win EVERYTHING, that being evil always prevails. You act like a good citizen, and you get shit on. That was how it felt. I just couldn't believe that this was happening to me. I still had to go to work. I was in debt. I had no money, my brain felt like it was no longer a part of me. I had gone back into a functional freeze. Feeling numb and dissociated from everything, I had gone into zombie mode internally. I struggled to take information in. I went into overdrive. Blocking out my trauma as best as I could. The same as I had done all my life during and after childhood sexual abuse. Patterns were reforming. Repeating themselves over and over. Here I am at 44, my first taste of abuse was at 6. That was 37 years of living in survival mode. Constant fight, flight and freeze. My whole life has been like this.

How was I not dead in a grave somewhere? How am I managing to claw myself out of bed every morning, putting on a face, looking fine to the outside world, but absolutely dying inside? My brain was mush but I had to keep showing the world I was fine. I had not taken time off work through it all. How the hell did I not take time off? I had gone through so much trauma yet; I didn't let anyone see what I was going through.

Even now, 5 years later I cannot comprehend how I had the strength to continue with life given all it had dealt me. Friends will often ask me how I manage. And I just don't have the answers. I just do – not – know and maybe I never will, not really.

My parents did help me as much as they felt they could. They put me and my son up until I sorted out accommodation for the two of us. They were never really ones to deal with stuff and I never felt emotionally that they were grasping what had happened. They just couldn't get it. I had dealt with it all emotionally by myself, so I continued to do this. I didn't tell them every little detail as I didn't feel like they understood and I had been programmed from a young age to deal with it all so this also became a pattern in every area of my life. People let me down. This is the narrative I had been left with. No one will look after me, so I must do it all alone. I didn't know any other way. I had done it all my life.

Remember, I had kept the abuse quiet about the first abuser, then the rest that followed.

The dirty old man at the clothes shop I worked in...

The dirty old curb crawlers that drove slowly beside me on the way home from my mates when I was a teenager.

The man who had financially abused me to protect his gambling addiction.

The man who controlled everything I did and said, where I went and how I dressed, what I ate...

The man who verbally, physically, emotionally, financially and sexually assaulted me. The rape he inflicted on me. The constant name-calling and derogatory comments.

The lack of help from the authority and, being called a liar. Followed by the feeling of being a failure because of all those things.

The judgement I felt from others when I had all this abuse. The way I got told I was a mug for putting up with it all and not walking away. The shame and guilt I felt about myself reinforced the things that others were saying. Often it wasn't meant from a mean place, but they were not educated in how to speak about this type of thing. Their language was totally misguided and incorrect. Nevertheless, hurtful.

# CHAPTER 13
# MOVING FORWARD

I was dealt such a horrific hand, just like many people have at the hands of the abusers. Something we as survivors would never want to have someone else going through, but it's a fact this happens. There are always going to be sick individuals who want to inflict pain and agony on others to make themselves feel powerful. To make themselves feel better and to soothe their own wounds, whether inflicted on them by others or by themselves.

We think these people have gotten away with things. It feels like they have had no punishment, but they will never be happy, because they are not happy with themselves. If someone is happy with themselves, why the fuck would they want to inflict this type of pain onto others.

*They* are cowards and will live a life of unhappiness mentally and emotionally, even when they look on the outside like they are living their best life. They know what they did and they will have to live with that.

Not many think of the grief you feel as a victim or survivor of childhood sexual abuse.

When you have lived in silence all of your life, you grieve the life you should have had. You mourn the little you whose childhood was cruelly taken away from them.

You grieve the adult you should have been allowed to turn into. The person you *wished* you may have been.

The sadness and anger of the injustice of it all. The loneliness and secrecy that clouded your life.

2 years ago, I told my parents about the abuse I suffered as a child but their reaction still baffles me today. They looked shocked to a point, but there was a significant lack of emotion.

No hugs, no tears, no warmth. I remember my dad saying how it all made sense now, but he didn't elaborate.

My mum kept asking me for specific details, like I had to explain every inch of what I suffered. They still speak to the childhood abuser. For decades I had to endure family parties and Christmases in the company of the abuser. I can only think that it was her way of having justification as to whether she mentioned or confronted the abuser or not. So, they could decide whether it was 'worth' tearing up the family by raising it with him.

They couldn't seem to grasp that the 'details' had been locked away for 40 years! To unlock this would be highly traumatic for me. Even when I told them I would not divulge any more than I already had, it was pursued. Completely dismissing my boundaries.

Over time, I couldn't be around them anymore. They just couldn't grasp it. They would only worry about how *they* felt about it all. Not how it had impacted me.

They brought up the conversation when they felt the need, but it was always when we were short of time. If I had to collect my son from a club or from friends. Never when we could take some time over it and this aggravated the hell out of me.

They always maintained they believed me, but not enough to do anything about it.

COVID had arrived and I really enjoyed that time. I enjoyed the isolation. Controversial I know, but for me, it meant I could feel what I needed to feel without having to put the mask on. I was relieved. Relieved that I got out of the domestic abuse, just before lockdown was inflicted on us.

I could then begin to mourn all that I had lost and it gave me time to put a plan together for my future.

I often hear you should forgive to move on. I don't necessarily agree with that. Why should you forgive the people that hurt you so fucking bad? NO.

Forgiveness is an individual choice. Never allow anyone; family, friends, or a faith say you have to forgive all of the wrongs in order to move on. I have lost all traces of hate, but for me, forgiveness is earned. Not just given. If you are a survivor reading this, you do what is right for *YOU*.

The people who inflicted harm will have their own penance to pay for their shitty behaviour. Not you.

I can move on now, because I know I am a good person, with a kind heart and a loving soul.

The abusers and their flying monkeys do not have a hold over me anymore and never will again.

**"Trauma creates change you don't choose.**
**Healing is about creating change you do choose"**
**- Michelle Rosenthal**

I am getting my power back.

I was introduced by a DV advocate to help a Charity called Healthwatch Essex with a pilot project they were working on. This is when I started my volunteering journey. Gradually, my worth started to grow and my whole outlook started to change.

The more I delved into my volunteering role, the more I was using my voice to educate and help others. Showing survivors that they are NEVER alone. Helping services understand how to improve the way they do things.

Feeling tired and sleep-deprived, I embarked on a meditation journey. I had never tried it before and I was sceptical of the help it may offer. Initially I would listen to a guided meditation to start with and I will be honest, I thought it was a load of crap, because every night I would listen with my earphones in whilst I was in my bed and I would hear every single bloody word. I would still be wide awake at the end of it. I was like ffs, what a load of shite ;)

But I persevered. I would say it started to kick in by about the third month of continually doing it. A breakthrough!! Finally, I started to notice that I had slowly begun to miss a bit of the ending and as I continued, less and less was being listened to consciously.

Over time, I started to reap the benefits. I finally found I was sleeping at night.

You never realise how important sleep is until you are deprived of it. Slowly, although still in fight or flight mode I started feeling slightly better, bit by bit.

I started looking into learning about my experiences. The more I learned the more I wanted to. I started to learn about narcissistic abuse from quite a well-known coach in this industry. My nan happened to pass away after the court case and she left me a little money in her will, which came around at the same time. This lady was talking about the training she provided and happened to be for the same amount too.

This *must* have been a sign, I thought. I would rather put my inheritance towards something worthwhile than just use it for more bills and, hopefully, would be able to form some sort of career from all my heartache. I would be able to turn my pain into purpose and help others who have gone through similar things I had.

There *HAD* to be some sort of light at the end of this dark, devastating tunnel. I had to do this, otherwise the perpetrators would have won. They walk away free as a bird, yet I live in this prison of injustice. I *cannot* and *will not* be a victim.

I became more confident in who I am as a person. I may still not be exactly where I want to be, but that is ok, because we are constantly evolving and growing.

Being strong in my story, and my truth.

No longer giving a flying fuck what people think. The shame is not mine to hold onto.

It is my duty as a WARRIOR to tell it. To be the voice for those who cannot YET.

To inspire others to share their stories when they are ready to.

For those wondering why they have suffered multiple abusive relationships.

To understand how the abuse had merged into other aspects of their lives.

I often asked in my story, 'Why is this happening to me?" The feeling of shame and guilt should have been laid on the shoulders of those who hurt me, including the justice system that let me down. I could have let this destroy me.

But I started to undergo counselling. We were chatting about decisions I was making in my adulthood and she turned to me and asked me a pivotal question:

**"Are you making that decision as the adult you are today, or are you making it as that little child?"**It sounded so simple, but it hadn't entered my mind until now. There was my 'aha' moment. Because suddenly it had become clear.

I had lived a lifetime of trauma through the lens of a child. My trauma was running the show. All the crap I had suffered was because of my beliefs, the beliefs handed down from my parents and the low self-esteem that had landed on my shoulders from my earliest memories. I wasn't aware of *how* to make logical congruent decisions, because everything I did came out of fear.

**I did what I did because I didn't know any other way.**

This for me finally connected all the dots. It put all the missing parts of me together. My inner child was doing her very best to love and protect me the only way she knew how.

NONE of the bad things had been *my* fault. I wasn't equipped to move my life into a different direction. I now realise the negative self-talk was fighting to keep me safe. From getting hurt further.

Other people were projecting their thoughts onto me to cover up who *they* were. The parts they didn't like about themselves. This had ***nothing*** to do with me!

Connecting the dots helped me see how generational trauma played its part too.

The emotional and psychological scars from past experiences, often experienced by our parents or grandparents, can influence our own thoughts, feelings, and behaviours, sometimes without us even realising it. The effects of trauma can be passed down from one generation to the next.

This cycle often leads to patterns of abuse that manifest in various aspects of life, particularly in relationships, which is how it was for me. I realise it has been essential for my healing to understand how this happens and how it shaped my adult experiences.

When someone experiences trauma of any kind, it can often create deep emotional wounds. If unresolved, they can affect how we interact with the world around us. We may struggle with trust or emotional regulation and may unintentionally pass on these struggles to our children through our behaviours, reactions, or even our parenting styles.

As children, we grow up observing and internalising our parents' responses to stress, conflict, and intimacy; we may adopt similar patterns, believing that these behaviours are normal or acceptable, often without conscious awareness.

Every thought and feeling I had was deeply influenced by my past experiences. I felt anxious during disagreements and would struggle to express my emotions openly and often shut down.

I learned to associate love with chaos or pain, so I unconsciously sought out partners who replicated that dynamic, perpetuating the cycle of abuse.

This extended to my decision-making too. I found myself drawn to familiar patterns, even when they were unhealthy. I was easily coerced and stayed in toxic relationships way longer than I should have.

I withdrew emotionally and found it difficult to build healthy connections, especially on a romantic level. These patterns created further isolation and misunderstanding, further complicating my ability to form meaningful relationships.

The trauma created invisible chains that bound me to patterns of abuse and unhealthy relationships, but by becoming aware of how my past shaped my present, I began to make conscious, informed choices.

I learned to communicate openly, setting boundaries, and understanding my emotional triggers. By acknowledging its impact on my thoughts, feelings, and decisions, I could take steps toward healing and breaking free from these cycles enabling me to build healthier relationships. I removed those who were no longer in alignment with me and this has been pivotal in leading a more fulfilling life and standing in my truth.

I became a Trauma Ambassador in 2020. I have attended lots of events, I have attended forums, I have co-produced a Trauma Card which has gone far further afield than we ever imagined. Helping thousands of people suffering from trauma, unable to speak out.

In April this year (2024), I was invited to speak with a journalist for the BBC!

This was aired on BBC news in May. I talked about my childhood trauma for the very first time. **40** years of silence and here I am talking about it on television!

I have trained for over four years in many healing modalities, making it my mission to help others to connect their own dots, by becoming a Childhood Trauma Coach, a Trauma Informed Narcissistic Abuse Specialist, Hypnotherapist, Master Reiki Practitioner and Energy Healer, helping others heal and thrive after a life of abuse.

Then of course this book!

**Finally** living my truth for all to see, no longer hiding, no longer ashamed of my past.

At 49, I am using my experiences to start living. I am so proud of who I am and how I turned my life around. Using this platform to disclose all I felt I had to hide.

I have met some beautiful and amazing fellow warriors from all over the world, united by our pains, but all aiming to make the world a better place.

Trauma didn't make me stronger, **I** MADE ME STRONGER.

It no longer defines me, but it is a small part of me.

Sometimes our unhealed trauma leads us down avenues we never thought we would be guided to. But it is through our healing that we begin to connect the dots and when we connect those dots, it alerts us to the root cause and now the deep healing can begin.

With knowledge comes power and with power comes purpose.

We can finally begin to lead the life we always deserved.

Lots of love and light,

Kari.

If you feel called to, please like and follow me. You can find me on Instagram: @heal_thrive_empower

Or have a look at my current Coaching and healing programs, if you would like to reach out.

Please go to: https://link.tree/healthriveempower

#connectingthedots

Printed in Great Britain
by Amazon

86272d11-534d-43b0-8783-f10e2390c811R01